KeyCHAMP

Technique Analysis • Speed Building

Walter M. Sharp, Ph.D.
Assistant Adjunct Professor of
Business and Office Education
The Ohio State University

Anthony A. Olinzock, Ph.D.
Professor of Business
and Office Education
The Ohio State University

Otto Santos, Jr., Ph.D.
Professor Emeritus of Business
and Office Education
The Ohio State University

SOUTH-WESTERN
THOMSON LEARNING

D1478066

Australia • Canada • Mexico • Singapore • Spain • United Kingdom • United States

SOUTH-WESTERN
™
THOMSON LEARNING

KeyChamp
By Walter M. Sharp, Anthony A. Olinzock, and Otto Santos, Jr.

Vice President/Executive Publisher:
Dave Shaut

Team Leader:
Karen Schmohe

Acquisitions Editor:
Jane Phelan

Project Manager:
Gayle Statman

Software Editor:
Mike Jackson

Production Editor:
Carol Spencer

Production Manager:
Tricia Boies

Executive Marketing Manager:
Carol Volz

Marketing Managers:
Nancy Long, Chris McNamee

Marketing Coordinator:
Cira Brown

Manufacturing Manager:
Charlene Taylor

Art and Design Coordinator:
Stacy Jenkins Shirley

Cover and Internal Design:
Joseph Pagliaro

Compositor:
Cover to Cover Publishing, Inc.

Printer:
Quebecor World/Dubuque

Rights and Permissions Manager:
Linda Ellis

WELCOME TO KEYCHAMP

KeyChamp is an exciting new software program designed to improve your keyboarding speed by analyzing your typing technique and prescribing practice that will help you key faster. *KeyChamp* is designed for those students who have learned the location of the keys on the keyboard and who now want to push themselves to become *champion* typists. Whether a beginning or advanced typist, you will find that this new program will help you achieve your fastest keyboarding speeds in the shortest possible time.

KeyChamp is based upon the fact that increasing the speed of your slowest two-letter keystroke combinations (*digraphs*) is the fastest way to gain overall keyboarding speed. In the past, it was necessary to key practice copy for long periods of time, without the knowledge of which digraphs were slow for you, until over time you practiced your slowest digraphs enough to improve your overall keyboarding speed. Why spend so much time keying without specific direction when *KeyChamp* can pinpoint your difficult digraphs and assign practice that will help you increase your speed?

Unlike most keyboarding software programs, *KeyChamp* does not emphasize typographical errors; rather the program focuses on what you've keyed correctly. Until now programs have limited technique analysis to words per minute and typographical errors. This limited analysis may lead to misdirected practice. *KeyChamp* analyzes your keyboarding technique by measuring your slowest digraphs and then assigns practice to speed them up. We believe accuracy is important, but we also believe that developing your maximum speed with an appropriate emphasis on accuracy is the primary objective. Accuracy is achieved after speed is maximized by reducing speed only one or two words a minute to obtain a *right speed*, a speed and accuracy rate as comfortable to you as writing with a pen or pencil.

Researchers have studied the relationship of digraphs to overall keyboarding speed since the twenties (Coover, 1923; Harding, 1933; Weitz and Fair, 1951; Nellermoe, 1965; Robinson, 1967; Beaumont, 1969; Olson, 1978; Erickson, 1979). Coover determined that expert typists key their slowest digraphs three times slower than their fastest digraphs. Harding found that highly skilled typists consistently keyed some digraphs slower and others faster. Because of the limitations of educational technology, these research findings were not largely applied in the traditional classroom.

However, in 1963, Walter M. Sharp, co-developer of the *KeyChamp* program, invented a device that measured hesitancies between keystrokes. Sharp discovered that he could help a student improve her speed by pulling typing paper through the typewriter at a constant pace, then studying the distance between the typed characters. (The machine invented to pull the paper through the typewriter became the Diatype.) Sharp learned that the student took too much time in operating the carriage return at the end of lines, thus slowing down her overall speed. Sharp studied the variable lines of typing by hundreds of other students, and he developed a skillbuilding system consisting of a three-point cycle: (1) analyze each two-letter combination (digraph) to find the slowest, (2) practice a drill containing the slow digraph, (3) measure skill progress by keying straight copy.

The *KeyChamp* program applies this practical three-point approach using the latest software and hardware technology. With his co-developers, Dr. Anthony Olinzock and Dr. Otto Santos, Sharp has developed the most advanced keyboarding software available. *KeyChamp* is simple to use. The complicated part of the program is inside the computer; the simple part is on the screen to teach you to key faster. If you have determination, you can reach your *champion* speed goal.

Contents

RECOMMENDED USE

KeyChamp may be used (1) as an individualized speed-building course, letting you work with the program for as long as it takes to achieve a desired speed or (2) jointly with *Century 21, Keyboarding & Information Processing, 6th Edition* or *College Keyboarding, 14th Edition*. The program can be used to grade and record evaluation timed writings from either the *KeyChamp* software or *Century 21/College Keyboarding* textbooks. In addition, the *KeyChamp* open screen word processor can be used to complete production work in *Century 21* or *College Keyboarding*. You may use the *KeyChamp* program any time after you have learned the alphabetic keys.

OVERVIEW

The *KeyChamp* software consists of 125 Sessions—100 Skillbuilding Sessions and 25 Assessment Sessions. Four Skillbuilding Sessions are followed by one Assessment Session, with this pattern repeating throughout the entire program. Each Skillbuilding Session consists of conditioning practice exercises and digraph analysis activities that help you focus on improving specific keyboarding skills. The Assessment Sessions are designed to measure the progress of your keyboarding speed and accuracy. A variety of performance records within the software display your progress as you complete the program. For your enjoyment, you can play the game *WordChamp* to celebrate the completion of each Session.

SKILLBUILDING SESSIONS

As you proceed through each Skillbuilding Session, the software analyzes your typing technique by precisely measuring the speeds of all two-keystroke combinations (or *digraphs*). A digraph speed is the *gwam* speed of any two-stroke combination, such as *th*. KeyChamp compares all of your digraph speeds to an acceptable norm and then assigns specific digraph drills for the slowest digraphs below your norm. Improving your slowest digraph speeds will increase your timed writing rate (*gwam*) as you progress through the program. In *KeyChamp*, digraphs are introduced in the order of most common to least common; thus, *th* and *he* appear in Session 1; *xf* and *xq* appear in Session 99.

Conditioning Practice

The Conditioning Practice (1) allows you to exercise and loosen the muscles by typing alphabetic sentences and (2) introduces you to the digraphs emphasized in the Session's Evaluation Analysis timed writing. You will key the two sets of copy at an *accuracy rate*, a *speed rate*, and a *control rate*. The three rates will be displayed on the screen. By the time you have completed all the Sessions, you will be introduced to 482 alphabetic digraphs in addition to the numbers and symbols.

Evaluation Analysis

The Evaluation Analysis section has a timed writing containing all the digraphs introduced in the Conditioning Practice. After you key the paragraph, *KeyChamp* will measure the speed of the designated Session digraphs as well as all other digraphs in the writing. It is possible that the particular digraphs introduced in a Session *may not* be a problem for you—*KeyChamp* will still find your slowest digraphs in the timed writing. *KeyChamp* provides the following information about your performance on the timed writing:

- Digraph Range—the fastest and slowest digraphs (reported in *gwam* rates) you keyed during the timed writing.

- Digraph Norm—(slowest digraph norm) the ideal or target rate (*gwam*) at which you should strive to key your slowest digraphs. The norm is determined by dividing your fastest digraph rate by three.

- Accuracy Percentage—should be 60% or better.

- Skill-Level—the *fastest* sixty-stroke string (*gwam*) you were able to key during the timed writing. Skill-Level should be above your *gwam* rate and should indicate a speed you are capable of keying for all your keyboarding in the near future.

- Typographical Errors—the keying errors you make, if any, during the timed writing are marked on your writing as follows:

Symbol	Description
⌐⌐	Transposed words
⌐	Transposed letters
/	Letter should be lowercase
∨	Missing letter, word(s), digit
⊔	Extra space (close up space)
≡	Letter should be uppercase
▨	Extra character, misspelled word, extra word, etc., are highlighted.

Depending upon your instructor's settings, the program may require that you key more than one timed writing. The results of the timed writing display a variety of information about the slowest digraphs you keyed; also, you may display or print a Digraph Chart.

Of critical importance is the information that compares your slowest digraphs in the writing with a norm expected of you at this stage of your keyboarding experience. Some digraphs will always be slower than others because of the location of the two keys on the keyboard, but there is a normal speed established for difficult digraphs below which your digraph speed may be too slow. The program assigns drills containing either your three slowest or three fastest digraphs for practice, depending on whether or not you keyed digraphs slower than your digraph norm.

Individualized Practice

You may practice a digraph drill with or without a pacer window. If you are not having trouble keeping your eyes on the copy, ask your teacher to set the program to display the drill without the pacer window. If you do have trouble keeping your eyes on the copy, use the pacer window. The window allows drill material to pass into view and out of view; thus, if you take your eyes off the copy you will miss portions of the copy. In either case the program will establish a speed goal after you have keyed the drill line the first time. On the next drill line, you should strive to key the copy at your goal rate. If you use the pacer window, it will move according to your goal rate. To complete a drill successfully, you must key at your goal rate with acceptable accuracy and, at least once, key the diagnosed digraph faster than you keyed it in the Evaluation Analysis timed writing. When you have successfully completed all the practice, you are ready to have some fun!

WordChamp

WordChamp is a word game that gives you a break after your hard speed-building work. You can even compete with other students in your class. Try to find as many words (3 or more letters in length) as possible in the time allowed. When time expires, the program automatically checks the words you entered and displays the points earned.

Only one word search puzzle is provided for each Session so that every student working in a Session will see exactly the same puzzle. This way, everyone has the same chance to win if you decide to compete against other students.

1. When you are ready, choose to begin the *WordChamp* game. (If you prefer, you can skip the game and proceed to the Progress Report.)

2. When the puzzle appears, find as many words as you can in the time allowed. Key the words in the area provided. You can separate each word by a space instead of placing each word on a new line.

RULES:

- Find words of three or more letters in length by connecting adjacent letters (horizontally, vertically, and diagonally) in any direction. For example, the words "tax" and "hat" are found in the sample puzzle shown below.

- You may use a particular cube only once to form any given word. For example, "that" is not allowed because you would need to use the cube with the letter "t" twice. If a game board contains two "t's" on different cubes, you may use both of these letters to form a word.

- You must spell words correctly. No points are awarded for misspelled words.

- Points are assigned based on the length of each word: three-letter words (one point), four-letter words (three points), five-letter words (five points), and so on.

- Proper names, hyphenated words, contractions, words considered foreign, and abbreviations are *not* allowed.

- No duplicate words are allowed.

3. Review your score and word list after time expires. Incorrect words and duplicates are marked with a red line through the word.

4. Click the **Print** button if you want to print the game report.

5. When time expires, your score will be automatically added to the top ten list if your score is one of the ten best.

Progress Report

The Skillbuilding Progress Report shows you how well you controlled the keying of a particular Session. An abbreviated report appears after you complete a Session. To display/print a comprehensive report, either click the **Print** button or choose *Progress Report* from the **Reports** menu. The comprehensive version for the Skillbuilding Sessions includes the following information:

- The rate (*gwam*) you keyed the Conditioning Practice lines, for accuracy, speed, and control.

- The rate (*gwam*) you keyed the Evaluation Analysis timed writings, the percent of accuracy, your skill level, the digraph range indicating the speed of your fastest and slowest digraph, and your digraph norm.

- The rate (*gwam*) of the ten slowest alphabetic digraphs, the slowest special reaches, and the digraphs emphasized in the Session. The special reach rates have been weighted to reflect the relative difficulty of these reaches compared to the al- phabetic reaches.

- The digraphs you keyed in the Individualized Practice.

- The number of minutes you played the game, the number of words found, and your total points.

ASSESSMENT SESSION

The Assessment Session timed writings measure the progress you have made to this point. Straight copy written to be of average difficulty is used. There is no emphasis upon any particular digraphs. This is the only section in the program in which grades are recorded.

Conditioning Practice

The Conditioning Practice consists of the alphabetic sentences from the previous four Sessions. Keying each sentence three times will prepare you for the Assessment timed writings. Your *accuracy rate, speed rate,* and *control rate* are displayed each time you complete a sentence.

Evaluation Progress

The material for the timed writings may be selected from the *KeyChamp* textbook or from *Century 21/College Keyboarding*. You may select a one-minute, two-minute, three-minute, or five-minute timed writing. When you complete each timed writing, your *gwam rate*, *accuracy*, and *skill-level* appear on the screen. To successfully complete the Session, you must key two timed writings. You may repeat the exercise until you are satisfied with your keying effort.

The following reports contain information from the Assessment Sessions.

- **Progress Report**—lists (1) *accuracy rate*, *speed rate*, and *control rate* of your Conditioning Practice, (2) the textbook used for each timed writing, along with the *length*, *speed*, *accuracy*, and *skill-level*, and (3) the number of minutes, words found, and total points from the game.

- **Assessment Performance Record**—lists information for all Assessment Sessions completed, including Session number, the date completed, whether or not the Conditioning Practice was completed, the length of the writing, the *gwam* rate, accuracy, and the scores for the *WordChamp* game. In addition, your speed and accuracy grade for each timed writing, length, and your overall course grades are listed.

Once you complete the Evaluation Progress section, you are ready to have some fun again by playing *WordChamp*!

OPEN SCREEN

The Open Screen is a word processor that includes numerous formatting options including fonts, styles, margins, tabs, justification, and line spacing. The Open Screen also provides a built-in timer for timed writings. Access Open Screen any time by clicking the **Open Screen** button. When you finish working with the Open Screen, save your work and choose *Exit Open Screen* from the **File** menu. You will use Open Screen for Speed Clinics and for *Century 21/College Keyboarding* lessons.

Speed Clinics

Each Session contains a Speed Clinic that provides a drill for each of the digraphs emphasized in the Session. You may want to practice your particularly difficult digraphs by keying Speed Clinic drills: (1) look up the digraph in the Digraph Index at the back of the book; (2) locate the Session that emphasizes that digraph; (3) go to that Session in the text and key the Speed Clinic drill lines that emphasize that digraph.

Century 21/College Keyboarding Lessons

You may use the Open Screen to key the early lessons that introduce the alphabetic keys prior to using *KeyChamp*. You may also key the production work of all your *textbook* lessons in the Open Screen option. The production work cannot be graded by the software, but it can be saved to your disk or printed. Timed writings keyed in the Open Screen are timed only; the software does not provide analysis in the Open Screen. If you want to analyze a timed writing for errors and *gwam*, return to an Assessment Session in the *KeyChamp* program.

DIGRAPH PRACTICE

As you progress through the *KeyChamp* program, you may find that certain digraphs could benefit from extra practice. Use the Digraph Practice screen to choose specific digraphs that *you* feel like practicing—choices include alphabetic digraphs, shift key, spacing, punctuation, numbers, and symbols. The results of drill lines keyed in the Digraph Practice section will not appear on any student or instructor reports. Access Digraph Practice by clicking on the **Digraph Practice** button from the main screen.

KeyChamp Sessions

The 125 Sessions of this program are arranged to progress through learning cycles consisting of 5 Sessions each. The first four Sessions of a cycle are for skillbuilding. The Skillbuilding Sessions consist of: (1) a Conditioning Practice for warm up and to introduce the digraphs to be tested, (2) an Evaluation Analysis with a timed writing to analyze your keyboarding technique (to determine your slowest digraphs), and (3) Individualized Practice, which consists of customized drills based upon the Evaluation Analysis. Every fifth Session is an Assessment Session containing a Conditioning Practice and two timed writings, which are evaluated to map your keyboarding progress. At the end of every Session you may play the game *WordChamp*.

Start-Up Procedures

KeyChamp begins with Skill Session 1; or, if you've already completed Sessions, *KeyChamp* will point you to the next incomplete Session. Follow the instructions given to you on the screen.

Session *1* — Skillbuilding

**1a ●
Conditioning
Practice**

Key the Alphabetic Practice and the Digraph Practice three times. The first time key the line at an *accuracy* rate emphasizing exactness. The second time key at a *speed* rate, trying to key as fast as your fingers can go. Finally, key a third time at a *control* rate, emphasizing a right speed for you using proper technique. Each time you complete the sentence, the speed results box indicates the GWAM you keyed. After you have completed the practice you will be asked, "Do you want to repeat the exercise?" Strike Y or N.

Alphabetic Practice
Jim found learning to be very quick and exciting; he was not a lazy person.

Digraph Practice (th in he re er ou es)
the math other inn main finds her then tithe red area aware era herb after you tour ounce yes pest acres

---

55. COMPUTER GRAPHICS

gwam 3'

For many years, people thought of a graphic as a hand-drawn	4	51
image or a picture on a page. Now that it is easy to obtain	8	55
graphics software for the personal computer, the situation has	12	59
changed. Graphics software provides a copy of an actual picture	17	63
or a drawing, or it will let the user finish a drawing by the use	21	68
of software tools. A photograph taken with a digital camera or	25	72
some other equipment is often used as a graphic. Text is also	30	76
easily added to a graphic. Different types of fonts are used for	34	81
this purpose. The use of graphics provides an opportunity for a	38	85
company to complete professional looking documents within the	42	89
company rather than paying an outside source for graphics work.	47	93

gwam 3' | 1 | 2 | 3 | 4 |

56. HARDWARE/SOFTWARE

gwam 3' | 5'

One of the first topics you will talk about in your personal	4	2	49
computer class is the difference between computer hardware and	8	5	51
software. Your teacher may tell you that the hardware consists	13	8	54
of the computer itself and all of the related physical equipment	17	11	56
that is needed for you to use the computer properly. Some of the	21	13	59
hardware you will find out about includes disk drives, keyboards,	26	15	61
modems, printers, and monitors. It is important that you learn	30	18	64
how to clean and care for all of your computer hardware. You	34	20	66
must also learn to properly turn on and off all of the equipment.	38	23	69
You will learn in class that computer software directs the	42	25	71
hardware to do its work in the proper way. You may already know	47	28	74
about a common type of software, a word processor. Other kinds	51	31	77
include database, spreadsheet, desktop publishing, and graphics.	55	33	79
Often these are included in one integrated package that is sold	60	36	82
at a very reasonable price. Software costs are most likely based	64	38	84
on the quality and quantity of work that the software will allow	68	41	87
a personal computer to do. It's very important that your hard-	72	43	90
ware have enough memory to run the software that you want to use.	77	46	92

gwam 3' | 1 | 2 | 3 | 4 |
      5' | 1 | 2 | 3 |

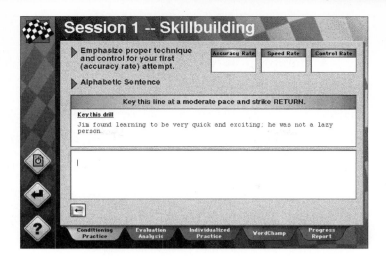

Ib • **E**

Evaluation ~ Analysis

Key the timed writing. When you strike the Tab key, timing will begin. When you have keyed all of the text press ENTER to end the timed writing. The time needed to strike Tab and ENTER will not be included when *KeyChamp* calculates your words a minute speed.

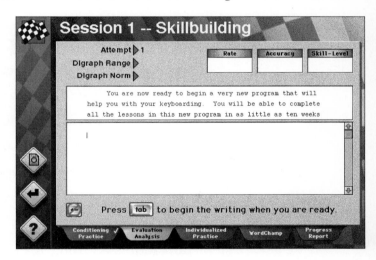

The difficulty index symbol (to the right of the Session part number) indicates the difficulty level of this timed writing (E for Easy, LA for Low Average, A for Average, HA for High Average, and D for Difficult). As you progress through the *KeyChamp* program, the difficulty level of the timed writings in the Skillbuilding Sessions will gradually increase from LA to D.

When you complete a timed writing, your Digraph Range, Slowest Digraph Norm, GWAM rate, Accuracy Percentage, and Skill-Level are indicated. Typographical errors are also marked. Depending on the settings set by your instructor, you may key the timed writing up to three times. When you complete all the timed writings you will be asked, "Do you want to repeat this exercise?" Strike Y or N.

Timed Writing

You are now ready to begin a very new program which will help you with your keyboarding. You will be able to complete all the lessons in this new program in as little as ten weeks or less. If you just complete each of the lessons with zeal, you will begin to see your skill grow very quickly.

53. WHAT IS A DATABASE?

gwam 3'

A database is a collection of information arranged for ease | 4 | 50
and speed to search or retrieve. It is mainly a list with infor- | 8 | 55
mation that may be used now or in the future. Think of a data- | 12 | 59
base as a filing cabinet with different types of information that | 17 | 63
is kept for present and future use. All types of small firms and | 21 | 68
individuals use the personal computer for managing a database. | 26 | 72
Larger computers are most likely used when the volume warrants | 30 | 76
them. At times, software for a database is used without any | 34 | 80
change made to it. In some cases, software is programmed for a | 38 | 84
specific type of database used in a firm. A database allows a | 42 | 89
user to easily choose only the information required as needed. | 46 | 93

gwam 3' | 1 | 2 | 3 | 4 |

54. ELECTRONIC MAIL

gwam 3' | 5'

Electronic mail, commonly referred to as E-mail, is often | 4 | 2 | 48
used as a fast and fun way to send and receive messages. The | 8 | 5 | 50
number of E-mail messages sent and received each day is amazing. | 12 | 7 | 53
E-mail may be used for personal and business purposes. If you | 17 | 10 | 55
use an Internet connection, E-mail does not often cost extra. | 21 | 13 | 58
Since it is so fast, E-mail is a great way to ask for information | 25 | 15 | 60
you need right away. To send and receive E-mail, you must have | 30 | 18 | 63
an address. Your E-mail address, like your postal address, must | 34 | 20 | 66
be unique.   Otherwise, someone else might get your messages. | 38 | 23 | 68

E-mail software is used to send and receive messages. Some | 42 | 25 | 71
software is free and may be downloaded from the Internet. There | 46 | 28 | 73
may be very little support or help for this kind of software. | 51 | 30 | 76
E-mail software is often included in the cost of an account with | 55 | 33 | 78
an Internet server, who is likely to provide good support and | 59 | 35 | 81
help for its software. E-mail software may be bought by itself. | 63 | 38 | 83
A firm that sells this software often provides good support in | 68 | 41 | 86
making sure it functions properly. With more and more practice, | 72 | 43 | 88
you will find that E-mail software is very easy to use. | 76 | 45 | 91

gwam 3' / 5' | 1 | 2 | 3 | 4 |

Ic ●
Individualized Practice

Key the drill line at a steady pace. After you have keyed a drill line once, your goal is established. You may change your goal by using the spin controls. To complete a drill successfully, you must key at your goal rate with acceptable accuracy and key the diagnosed digraph (at least once) faster than you keyed it in the Evaluation Analysis timed writing. When you successfully complete the drill you will be asked "Do you want to repeat the exercise?" Strike Y or N.

Id ●
WordChamp

The object of the game is to find as many words (3 or more letters in length) as possible in the time allowed. When time expires, the program automatically checks the words you enter and displays the points earned.

Only one word search puzzle is provided for each Session so that every student working in a Session will see exactly the same puzzle. If you have any questions about the rules of the game turn to pages ix-x in the Introduction before playing the game or access the program's Help file.

Ie ●
End of Class Procedure

If you are not continuing to the next Skill Session at this time, complete the following steps:

- Exit the program.
- If you are using disks, remove them and store them properly.
- Turn off the computer and, if applicable, the printer.

51. SPREADSHEET SOFTWARE

gwam 3'

A spreadsheet has rows and columns of numbers. It also has	4	50
formulas to do various types of calculations. You can easily	8	54
change the formula, add data, or make corrections. If one or	12	58
more items are changed in a spreadsheet, new results are auto-	16	62
matically figured. You can create bar, pie, and line charts	20	66
of your data with most spreadsheet software. Because of the	25	70
large amount of time required and the need for accuracy, use the	29	75
most up-to-date software and the fastest personal computer that	33	79
you can afford. These types of programs are often part of a	37	83
larger suite of programs that may also include a database, a word	42	87
processor, and maybe even a program for creating presentations.	46	92

gwam 3' | 1 | 2 | 3 | 4 |

52. INVESTMENT GOALS

gwam 3' | 5'

Investing is a process that often requires sound research	4	2	48
and expert advice. People have many ways to invest. Real	8	5	50
estate, gold, and silver are only a few types of investments.	12	7	53
Stocks and bonds are very popular. A person may buy stocks and	16	10	55
bonds through mutual funds, or they may be bought directly.	20	12	58
Often people invest in pension plans. Many times these plans are	25	15	60
used over several years with proceeds that often start at the	29	17	63
time a person retires. Social security is also a popular kind of	33	20	65
investment. The benefits often add to a plan for retirement.	38	23	68
The goals of individuals often determine the different types	42	25	70
of investments that are made. These goals may vary during the	46	28	73
life of a person; thus the investments may also vary from time to	50	30	76
time. Frequently, people have one or two primary goals in mind	55	33	78
or a combination of the two. One of these goals is that of hav-	59	35	81
ing a secure investment. This may mean less return and probably	63	38	83
less increase in the value of the investment. Another goal is to	67	40	86
invest at a higher risk to realize a greater return, but indi-	72	43	88
viduals should never invest more than they can afford to lose.	76	45	91

gwam 3' | 1 | 2 | 3 | 4 |
5' | 1 | 2 | 3 |

Speed Clinic

The following drills contain the digraphs emphasized in this Session. Practice them on the Open Screen when you would like extra practice on particular digraphs. The drills will not be analyzed or recorded by the *KeyChamp* program.

My mother saw three tooth marks on the fourth finger. After the injury she made an inquiry for the court.

Father plans to retire and live on the regal estate where he can raise wheat.

th	them thin three theme other mother months tooth math fourth
in	inns inner injury inquiry king line pink pint join main pain
he	hen heels heard hearts held wheat these shelf mother she the
re	reel regal relax reduce retire scream scare share stress are
er	era erased govern ever fever linger folder her hunter hunger
ou	outs outset about account count court proud pour foul fourth
es	escort estates esteem best west test west yes eyes sees toes

Refer to page **R-1** for tips on efficient keying of individual letters.

49. WORD PROCESSING

gwam 3'

Preparing text is very different now than in the past. For	4 | 50
example, words that were recorded at slow rates through writing	8 | 55
by hand or keying on a typewriter can now be processed at a very	13 | 59
fast rate by use of the personal computer. Various up-to-date	17 | 63
software programs for word processing are now in use with the	21 | 67
personal computer. These programs allow for very fast input and	25 | 72
checking for errors in spelling and grammar. Work with tables,	30 | 76
envelopes, and labels is made easier. A printout is made pos-	34 | 80
sible by a combination of software and a printer that results in	38 | 84
mailing quality, if desired. In our world today, the use of up-	42 | 89
to-date word processing is basic to a good communication system.	46 | 93

gwam 3' | 1 | 2 | 3 | 4 |

50. TAKE-HOME SALARY

gwam 3' | 5'

You either have had or will have a great shock when you re-	4	2 | 48
ceive your first take-home salary. Hopefully, you have not pre-	8	5 | 50
pared a budget based on your gross salary. The amount of your	12	7 | 53
take-home salary likely is smaller than you expected. Because	17	10 | 56
of certain deductions, you will discover that the gross amount of	21	13 | 58
your salary changes. These deductions are generally a result of	25	15 | 61
local, state, and federal tax laws. With greater income and	29	18 | 63
lower number of exemptions, the higher is the amount deducted.	34	20 | 66
Check for errors to make sure that the net salary is correct.	38	23 | 68
The exact amount that is deducted from a salary varies among	42	25 | 71
people. For example, the income tax for state and local purposes	46	28 | 73
may vary depending on your location. Usually, you can count on	50	30 | 76
social security tax as a deduction. Health and life insurance	55	33 | 78
deductions are often shared with an employer. At times, a person	59	35 | 81
may have money deducted on a regular basis from a credit union.	63	38 | 84
Also, most types of retirement plans require a large deduction	68	41 | 86
from your salary, which is often tax deferred. Once you retire,	72	43 | 89
you have to pay income tax on any of the tax-deferred proceeds.	76	46 | 91

gwam 3' | 1 | 2 | 3 | 4 |
5' | 1 | 2 | 3 |

2a •
**Conditioning
Practice**

Key the Alphabetic Practice and Digraph Practice lines three times. The first time, key at an *accuracy* rate; the second time at a *speed* rate, and the third time at a *control* rate. Each time you complete the sentence, the speed results box indicates the GWAM you keyed. After you have completed the practice you will be asked, "Do you want to repeat the exercise?" Strike Y or N.

Alphabetic Practice
Pam W. Zack quickly got her very first job on her sixteenth birthday.

Digraph Practice (an on at or en ti)
any sang began one bone button attend fate wheat order sort for end rent alien tie stir until

2b • **E**
**Evaluation ~
Analysis**

Key the timed writing. When you strike the Tab key, timing will begin. When you have keyed all of the text press ENTER to end the timed writing. The time needed to strike Tab and ENTER will not be included when *KeyChamp* calculates your words a minute speed.

When you complete a timed writing, your Digraph Range, Slowest Digraph Norm, GWAM rate, Accuracy Percentage, and Skill Level are indicated. Typographical errors are also marked. Depending on the settings set by your instructor, you may key the timed writing up to three times. When you complete all the timed writings you will be asked, "Do you want to repeat this exercise?" Strike Y or N.

Timed Writing

When you complete this new program, you can expect to see your speed level increase as much as ten words per minute or more. Many of the errors that you make over and over again will also be gone. As you use this program, you will watch your skill grow with time.

2c •
**Individualized
Practice**

Key the drill line at a steady pace. After you have keyed a drill line once, your goal is established. You may change your goal by using the spin controls. To complete a drill successfully, you must key at your goal rate with acceptable accuracy and key the diagnosed digraph (at least once) faster than you keyed it in the Evaluation Analysis timed writing. When you successfully complete the drill you will be asked "Do you want to repeat the exercise?" Strike Y or N.

47. EARNING A PROMOTION

gwam 3'

What do you know about promotions in the world of business?   4 | 51

First, promotions often take place, and they occur for varied   8 | 55

reasons.   Second, promotions are not often automatic; rather they   13 | 59

must be earned by hard and honest work for a firm.   Third, pro-   17 | 63

motions very often result in an increase in salary, a change in   21 | 67

title, and a different series of tasks on a job.   Fourth, promo-   25 | 72

tions are often earned by persons who project good knowledge and   30 | 76

skills as employees on the job.   Fifth, promotions may require   34 | 80

moving to other geographic locations.   In summary, there is much   38 | 85

to know about promotions, but knowing a great deal about a job   42 | 89

and having good working skills are key to getting a promotion.   46 | 93

gwam 3' | 1 | 2 | 3 | 4 |

48. LISTENING TO MUSIC

gwam 3' | 5'

What kinds of music do you prefer to listen to?   It appears   4 | 2 | 48

that every era has its own style of music.   You might prefer more   8 | 5 | 50

than one kind of music and even dislike other kinds.   Your indi-   13 | 8 | 53

vidual taste might well determine the kinds of music that you   17 | 10 | 55

like or dislike.   There is loud music, soft music, or music in   21 | 13 | 58

between.   To a great extent, individuals tend to prefer music   25 | 15 | 60

that they heard when they were young.   You often find that others   30 | 18 | 63

also prefer your favorite kinds of music.   However, you probably   34 | 20 | 66

have certain music scores that are your personal favorites.   38 | 23 | 68

There are varied ways of listening to music.   Television and   42 | 25 | 71

radio are popular, as are various devices for listening to re-   46 | 28 | 73

corded music.   A concert by a group or an individual seems popu-   50 | 30 | 75

lar almost all of the time.   Taking part in some type of musical   54 | 33 | 78

group also helps you both hear and enjoy music.   As we listen to   59 | 35 | 81

music, we might marvel at the professional musician who through   63 | 38 | 83

years of hard work can create music that will live for a long pe-   67 | 40 | 86

riod.   Surely, life would be less enjoyable if we did not have a   72 | 43 | 88

chance to experience listening to our favorite kind of music.   76 | 45 | 91

gwam 3' | 1 | 2 | 3 | 4 |
        5' | 1 | 2 | 3 |

2d ●
WordChamp

If you have any questions about the rules of the game turn to pages ix-x in the Introduction before playing the game or access the program's Help file.

2e ●
End of Class Procedure

If you are not continuing to the next Skill Session at this time, complete the following steps:

- Exit the program.
- If you are using disks, remove them and store them properly.
- Turn off the computer and, if applicable, the printer.

Speed Clinic

The following drills contain the digraphs emphasized in this Session. Practice them on the Open Screen when you would like extra practice on particular digraphs. The drills will not be analyzed or recorded by the *KeyChamp* program.

I put my money in the bank every month. Athletic people can enjoy an active life even in retirement.

The artists ordered ten oranges and an entire order of beans for the banquet next month.

an	an and angel animal band bank brand cane mean organs veteran
on	on once one ones only none month money phone moon motion son
at	at ate atlas atoms athletic bath eats data date eat hat meat
or	or orbit order organ orange born cord lord door actor mirror
en	end enjoy entry enter entire bend lend pens hen men ten open
ti	tin tip till time tire title stir patio artist active retire

> Refer to page **R-1** for tips on efficient keying of individual letters.

45. OWNER OR EMPLOYEE?

As you consider a future in business think about these ques-	4	50
tions: First, would you aspire to own your own business someday?	8	54
Second, would you prefer the status of an employee, where you	13	59
will work for someone else? Also, you need to know that failure	17	63
rates are high for new businesses and that finding working capi-	21	67
tal is often a big challenge. Although the risk may be higher	25	71
for a business owner, the monetary gains and rewards may be much	30	76
greater than for an employee. If you work full-time for a busi-	34	80
ness you will gain some benefits, such as insurance. After com-	38	84
pleting a large amount of research, you will be able to decide	42	88
between owning your own business or becoming an employee.	46	92

gwam 3' | 1 | 2 | 3 | 4 |

46. COMPETITION AND YOU

Most individuals have competed in a class activity or a	4	2	47
sporting event. During a class, competition often develops when	8	5	50
you are ranked with others in some type of activity. During a	12	7	52
game in a sporting event, competition occurs between individuals	17	10	55
or teams. As you compete, the way you respond to others often	21	13	57
shows much about you as a person. Whether your team wins or	25	15	60
loses, the response you give to your own members and to those on	29	18	62
the other side should be positive. If you compete in a sporting	34	20	65
event as an individual, this type of attitude is also needed.	38	23	67
One of the most common types of competition involves com-	41	25	70
peting with yourself. You should attempt to do your best at all	46	27	72
times so that once the competition is completed, you can honestly	50	30	75
believe that you gave your best whether you performed as an	54	32	77
individual or as a member of a team. Competing with yourself can	59	35	80
assist you in determining how much you are improving from one	63	38	82
period of time to the next. Although it is exciting to be a win-	67	40	85
ner, it is often more rewarding to hear someone say that you dem-	71	43	88
onstrated your best ability while the game was played.	75	45	90

gwam 3' | 1 | 2 | 3 | 4 |
5' | 1 | 2 | 3 |

Session 3 — Skillbuilding

3a ●
Conditioning Practice

Key the Alphabetic Practice Sentence and the Digraph Practice three times—at an *accuracy* rate, a *speed* rate, then a *control* rate. After you have completed the practice you will be asked, "Do you want to repeat the exercise?" Strike Y or N.

Alphabetic Practice
Parker M. Walsh realized exactly four quarts might be available in June.

Digraph Practice (nd te to ur it ha st)
bends kind tea dated vote top autos into urge curve fur it cited quit had that alpha stay hasty best

---

3b ● Ⓔ
Evaluation ~ Analysis

Key the timed writing. When you strike the Tab key, timing will begin. When you have keyed all of the text press ENTER to end the timed writing. Depending on the settings set by your instructor, you may key the timed writings up to three times.

When you complete all the timed writings you will be asked, "Do you want to repeat this exercise?" Strike Y or N.

Timed Writing

How much time will it take you to key at a faster rate? The answer to that question will depend on you. You can't be lazy; just practice each day. Give yourself a chance to excel; practice each day.

3c ●
Individualized Practice

Key the drill line at a steady pace. After you have keyed a drill line once, your goal is established. You may change your goal by using the spin controls. To complete a drill successfully, you must key at your goal rate with acceptable accuracy and key the diagnosed digraph (at least once) faster than you keyed it in the Evaluation Analysis timed writing. When you successfully complete the drill you will be asked "Do you want to repeat the exercise?" Strike Y or N.

43. ACCOUNTING ON COMPUTERS

gwam 3'

	4	51

The personal computer is often used to record, summarize, and analyze accounting data for a firm. The size of a firm and the type and number of transactions often dictate the requirements for the personal computer and software that are used. For example, in smaller firms one computer is often used for all of the input and output of data. In larger firms a network system is often used. This system allows two or more personal computers to be linked together for the input and output of data. Because of the need for unique accounting functions, software is at times programmed for specific use by a firm. In other cases, some type of generic accounting software is purchased for use by a firm.

	3'	
	4	51
	8	55
	12	59
	17	63
	21	68
	25	72
	30	76
	34	81
	38	85
	43	89
	47	94

gwam 3' | 1 | 2 | 3 | 4 |

44. YOUR INSURANCE NEEDS

gwam 3' | 5'

Why do you think insurance is needed? First, it is a tool to reduce losses as a result of specific happenings that are not presently anticipated. Some examples are loss of life, health problems, fire, hail, floods, and auto accidents. Second, insurance is a tool to provide financial security. You need to think of only one major disaster to discern that financial security might be lost without insurance. Third, insurance allows you to have peace of mind. To know that you are able to replace or at least partially replace a potential loss gives peace of mind.

Insurance takes many forms. The many types of insurance available may confuse a person or a family seeking coverage. It is a good idea to talk with other people you trust to find out what kinds of insurance they have. Reliable and honest agents from varied insurance firms may also be of great help. Shop for insurance just as you shop for other kinds of goods and services. Health, property, and life insurance are some main kinds of insurance that need attention. Although families may differ in the amount of coverage, everyone needs certain kinds of insurance.

	3'	5'	
	4	2	48
	8	5	51
	13	8	53
	17	10	56
	21	13	58
	25	15	61
	30	18	63
	34	20	66
	38	23	68
	42	25	71
	46	28	73
	50	30	76
	54	33	78
	59	35	81
	63	38	83
	67	40	86
	72	43	89
	76	46	91

gwam 3' | 1 | 2 | 3 | 4 |
5' | 1 | 2 | 3 |

3d ●
WordChamp

If you have any questions about the rules of the game turn to pages ix-x in the Introduction before playing the game or access the program's Help file.

3e ●
End of Class Procedure

If you are not continuing to the next Skill Session at this time, complete the following steps:

- Exit the program.
- If you are using disks, remove them and store them properly.
- Turn off the computer and, if applicable, the printer.

Speed Clinic

The following drills contain the digraphs emphasized in this Session. Practice them on the Open Screen when you would like extra practice on particular digraphs. The drills will not be analyzed or recorded by the *KeyChamp* program.

How many items did they list on the itinerary? I wonder why the demand for the bus tour is under our estimate.

Stacey urged them to get the sea charts and itemize the list of changes before the next storm hits the channel.

nd	ends bonds hands kinds under wonder and end bond find demand
te	tea ten team tear teen tell item stem step elite quite white
to	to too toll took tour toast stop autos stocks to onto tomato
ur	urge urban urgent burn cure hurt jury sure fur our four hour
it	its itch item itself bite city site with fit hit sit suit
ha	had ham has hat hay hair than that what perhaps orphan alpha
st	star stay stem step stop rests costs lists chest beast waist

Refer to page R-1 for tips on efficient keying of individual letters.

E

41. VALUING FRIENDSHIPS

gwam 3'

	3'	
One of your goals should be to strive to be liked and not to	4	50
be disliked. This means that you must treat others as you would	8	55
like them to treat you. Even though this attempt does not guar-	13	59
antee success in developing friendships, it greatly increases	17	63
your chances to find rewarding relationships. If you genuinely	21	67
desire to like others with whom you associate, the results are	25	71
often very effective. You need to value those you care about and	30	76
endeavor to give to others as well as to receive from others.	34	80
You should not assume that friendships occur without efforts on	38	84
your part. You need to nurture friendships. A friendship nur-	42	88
tured over a long period will often remain over the years.	46	92

gwam 3' | 1 | 2 | 3 | 4 |

42. LAW ENFORCEMENT

gwam 3' | 5'

	3'	5'	
Why do we need law enforcement in our society? When you	4	2	47
really think about this question, you do not arrive at any simple	8	5	50
answers. We often think first of some crime that has been com-	12	7	52
mitted that requires action by the police. This is only one	16	10	55
small phase of law enforcement. In a broader sense, almost any-	21	12	57
thing we do and say has some bearing on the law. Thus, we should	25	15	60
perceive law enforcement as essential for an orderly society. It	29	18	63
should also foster fairness to all persons in our society. Think	34	20	65
about the alternatives in our nation without law enforcement.	38	23	68
Law enforcement takes different forms. In addition to pro-	42	25	70
tection from crime, law enforcement may assist in the personal	46	28	73
and business aspects of your life. For example, if you assume	50	30	76
that you have a case, you have the privilege to take your diffi-	54	33	78
culty to a small claims court or even much higher. If you do	59	35	80
require legal aid, you may need to secure competent counsel to	63	38	83
establish your part, if any, in an incident that could involve	67	40	85
the law. Thus, you have the right to a system of law enforce-	71	43	88
ment that attempts to protect you in varied legal situations.	75	45	90

gwam 3' | 1 | 2 | 3 | 4 |
5' | 1 | 2 | 3 |

4a ●
Conditioning Practice
Key each exercise at the right three times.

Alphabetic Practice
Patty Morrow recognized her request asked for leave from her job about six.

Digraph Practice (nt is ed of ar ng)
nth wants dent isn't miss tis edit medial red off soft proof are bear bar ngwee angle king

4b ● E
Evaluation ~ Analysis
Key the timed writing at the right.

Timed Writing
Learning to key in class will help you realize your career goal. Most of the jobs in the business world today will require that you key on the job. The time used to practice in class each day to learn to keyboard is an investment in your future.

4c Individualized Practice
Key the drill according to the prompts on your screen.

4d WordChamp
Play the game WordChamp.

4e End of Class Procedure . . .
if you are not continuing to the next Session.

Speed Clinic

My aunt spent all her rent on the tennis event. Twenty tied the county record for the island events. Wait for my proof.

Ed named the ten best officers to wear the red gear. Orange is the color for the new year. He hired an officer to help.

nt   into onto unto cents month tenth aunt cent dent event recent

is   is isles issue island disc dish fish list his this emphasis

ed   edge edit edges editor beds feeds media needs bed feed typed

of   of off offer office soft coffee layoff profit hereof whereof

ar   are arm art arch area army bare barn cart bar car ear collar

ng   angel angle angry range rings gang hang king long lung being

Refer to page R-1 for tips on efficient keying of individual letters.

39. MONEY AND YOUR LIFE

gwam 3'

A common way to define money is that it is a medium of 4 | 50
exchange. Although money is very significant, there are indi- 8 | 54
viduals who insist that money is the most essential element in 12 | 58
their lives. Do you reject this belief? Would you rather have a 16 | 62
healthy body and a sound mind than to have money? Would you 20 | 66
rather have good friends and those who care for you than to save 25 | 71
money? Would you rather be respected and admired by others than 29 | 75
to spend money? Your reaction to these and related questions de- 33 | 79
notes your value system. This does not mean that you cannot have 38 | 84
a suitable balance. Once you attain the desirable balance in 42 | 88
your value system, hopefully you will properly use your money. 46 | 92

gwam 3' | 1 | 2 | 3 | 4 |

40. PAYING YOUR TAXES

gwam 3' | 5'

Several distinct taxes exist. One primary tax is the income 4 | 2 | 48
tax. This tax is levied on the national level and frequently by 8 | 5 | 50
states and lower levels of government. The income tax is a prog- 13 | 8 | 53
ressive tax because the rates increase as adjusted gross income 17 | 10 | 55
of the taxpayer increases. The sales tax is frequently levied on 21 | 13 | 58
state and local levels but not at the national level. The sales 26 | 15 | 61
tax is a proportional tax because the rates do not normally fluc- 30 | 18 | 63
tuate on totals of sales. For persons who are at a low income 34 | 21 | 66
level, the proportional tax is considered regressive in nature. 38 | 23 | 68

Why do we pay taxes? Taxes are paid for varied reasons. 42 | 25 | 71
Money to operate agencies of the government is secured with 46 | 28 | 73
taxes. Taxes often provide funds for education. Further, taxes 51 | 30 | 76
protect us against crime. Highways are funded by the use of 55 | 33 | 78
taxes. The national forests and many of our lakes are often 59 | 35 | 80
taken care of with the collection of tax money. You may wisely 63 | 38 | 83
choose to define taxes as a way of sharing. Although we alone 67 | 40 | 86
cannot provide the many services desired by society, this is 71 | 43 | 88
often feasible by sharing our money through taxes with others. 75 | 45 | 91

gwam 3' | 1 | 2 | 3 | 4 |
      5' | 1 | 2 | 3 |

Session 5—Assessment

5a •
Conditioning Practice
Key the exercise at the right three times.

Alphabetic Practices
Jim found learning to be very quick and exciting; he was not a lazy person.

Pam W. Zack quickly got her very first job on her sixteenth birthday.

Parker M. Walsh realized exactly four quarts might be available in June.

Patty Morrow recognized her request asked for leave from her job about six.

5b •
Evaluation ~ Progress
Key the first timed writing at the right.

Timed Writing
Can you think of the kinds of records a business will need to keep? Which business will be asking for a record? Whose job will it be to organize and examine the records? This is quite a list of questions to be answered. The challenge is very great. Just be prepared to meet the demand.

5c •
Evaluation ~ Progress
Key the second timed writing at the right.

5d •
WordChamp
Play the game WordChamp.

Timed Writing
Group thinking is good only to the extent that personal thinking is useful. Each of us must have some idea of how we can help with the job to be done. The quick way to realize success is by using teamwork. Can you think of a time when using it was a success? Did you like it?

5e •
End of Class Procedure . . .
if you are not continuing to the next Skill Session.

Balanced-Hand Words

May she and I add these to the work list: visual aid, vial, visual field, workbox, wheelchair?

When did he yell for the batter to go to the end of the bag?

Go to a shanty and rub soap on the six wheels for the widow.

aid air aisle also bib bicycle bid big body chair chant chap

dial did die dig digit eight eighth eighty fib field flannel

giant giggle girl girls gland glee hair hale half halls halt

iambic ibid ibis icicle jake jam jams jangle dale kayak keel

laid lair laity lake lamb lame maid make male mall malt name

naps nape naught naughty nay oak oboe odd odor off of pajama

37. MAKING DECISIONS

gwam 3'

Do you like or dislike making decisions on a regular basis?	4 | 51
Whether you readily want to admit it, you are a decision maker.	8 | 55
The types of decisions you will make vary in terms of their mag-	13 | 59
nitude. Magnitude is determined by the nature of the decision	17 | 63
and by how many people the decision might affect. Further, you	21 | 68
are a decision maker even when you have to deal with decisions	25 | 72
made by others. If you like to make decisions, you may be inter-	30 | 76
ested in a management position. If not, you may choose another	34 | 81
level and serve as a receiver who carries out certain decisions.	38 | 85
You are often both a decision maker and a decision receiver. You	43 | 89
must learn to cope well with either one of these positions.	47 | 93

gwam 3' | 1 | 2 | 3 | 4 |

38. YOUR CREDIT UNION

gwam 3' | 5'

Employees often take advantage of the services offered by	4 | 2 | 47
credit unions in their firms. A credit union is often used by an	8 | 5 | 50
employee who wants to borrow, invest, or save. In some ways, a	13 | 8 | 53
credit union has services similar to a small bank or savings and	17 | 10 | 55
loan association. However, a credit union is owned by its em-	21 | 13 | 58
ployees. Credit unions differ from most banks in that they do	25 | 15 | 60
not offer as many services. Also, credit unions, which stress	29 | 18 | 63
short-term loans to consumers, differ from savings and loan as-	34 | 20 | 65
sociations, which stress long-term loans on real estate.	37 | 22 | 67
Credit unions often have lower overhead costs than firms	41 | 25 | 70
that offer short-term loans and savings accounts. As a result of	45 | 27 | 72
lower costs and the ease of receiving payments, interest on loans	50 | 30 | 75
is often lower than those of other kinds of firms having these	54 | 32 | 77
types of services. Also, the interest paid on savings is often	58 | 35 | 80
higher. An employee is often allowed to have a set amount with-	63 | 38 | 83
held from payroll checks to collect on loans or to receive as	67 | 40 | 85
savings. To protect the employee, a credit union has the same	71 | 43 | 88
governmental insurance plans on funds deposited as other firms.	75 | 45 | 90

gwam 3' | 1 | 2 | 3 | 4 |
5' | 1 | 2 | 3 |

Session 6 — Skillbuilding

6a ●
Conditioning Practice

Key each exercise at the right three times.

Alphabetic Practice
Many judges will keep the size of bail equal to half the court expenses involved.

Digraph Practice (se yo ve co io de fo)
sew buses wise you mayor embryo ever ovens cove cow score tobacco ion lion polio debt cadet ade fox afoul

6b ● E
Evaluation ~ Analysis

Key the timed writing at the right.

Timed Writing
Each day of the week many men and women go to work in the offices of this nation and have to use different types of office equipment and skills. These men and women have learned to use these skills and equipment in classes at high schools and colleges just as you are doing. If you want to achieve success, take pride and work very hard in class each day to strive for your career goal.

6c Individualized Practice
Key the drill according to the prompts on your screen.

6d WordChamp
Play the game WordChamp.

6e End of Class Procedure ...
if you are not continuing to the next Session.

Speed Clinic

I see four cases of roses. The order was for forty cases of roses. You can trade before the mayor and the aide arrives.

I need coal before it becomes too cold for the lion and cow.

se see set sew sex seal roses upset loser cases hose horse rose

yo you your young yours youth mayor rayon anyone layover embryo

ve vent very veto verbal even ever over cover five gave believe

co cow coal coat coin cold come cool score scout become tobacco

io ion ionizing lion riots action junior motion union portfolio

de desk depot dead dear deer cadet index order aide blade trade

fo for fox food fort four foul force forty afford before effort

Refer to page **R-1** for tips on efficient keying of individual letters.

35. SELECTING A CAREER

gwam 3'

When you consider future opportunities, you may tend to pick	4	51
diverse career paths. This is good because all people do not at-	8	56
tempt to reach out for the same opportunities. First, you might	13	60
want to think about your interests--your personal feelings toward	17	64
opportunities open to you. Second, you might want to think about	22	69
your aptitude--what you have the ability to do. If you consider	26	73
these two areas carefully and find a career that really does suit	30	77
you, you may increase your chances for a happy work life. How-	34	82
ever, as you gain more work experience and as your personal life	39	86
changes, you may need to reconsider your choice of a career.	43	90
Many people change careers at least once during their lifetime.	47	94

gwam 3' | 1 | 2 | 3 | 4 |

36. BORROWING MONEY

gwam 3' | 5'

Once you have borrowed, a debt is established that must be	4	2	48
repaid. Principal is the amount owed on a debt. Interest is the	8	5	50
amount that you pay on a debt for borrowing. You may borrow from	13	8	53
banks, small finance companies, credit unions, and other varied	17	10	56
sources. When payments are made on credit card purchases, inter-	21	13	58
est is typically paid on the unpaid balance each month. You need	26	15	61
to try to find the lowest interest rate. The law requires the	30	18	63
one from whom you borrow to indicate the actual interest rate	34	20	66
that is charged. Thus, you should know the cost of borrowing.	38	23	68
On what basis can a person borrow? You are limited on how	42	25	71
much you can borrow by differing factors, such as character, ca-	46	28	73
pacity, and collateral. Character is defined by how good your	51	30	76
reputation is and how honest you are in paying back your other	55	33	78
debts. Capacity is the ability to earn enough money to pay the	59	35	81
principal and the interest when they are due. Collateral is what	63	38	83
you own that may have to stand good for the amount borrowed.	68	41	86
Whatever your status, do not borrow unless you have ways and	72	43	88
means for repaying the amount of principal and interest owed.	76	45	91

gwam 3' | 1 | 2 | 3 | 4 |
5' | 1 | 2 | 3 |

Session 7 — Skillbuilding

7a •
Conditioning Practice

Key each exercise at the right three times.

Alphabetic Practice
Wan was very quick to object; he realized the taxi fare might possibly be high.

Digraph Practice (al le me as ll ce)
all bald call let bales male men comet fame ask phase seas llama rally all cent excel ace

7b • Ⓔ
Evaluation ~ Analysis

Key the timed writing at the right.

Timed Writing
You must be able to key if you want to use many types of office equipment. You must practice to learn to key at your fastest speed. If you key at a fast rate, you will change the output of your office. Your skill to key can help you realize your goal of an exciting career.

7c Individualized Practice
Key the drill according to the prompts on your screen.

7d WordChamp
Play the game WordChamp.

7e End of Class Procedure . . .
if you are not continuing to the next Session.

Speed Clinic

When the alert sounds go to the cellar and wait for the bell to ring. Sometimes you can smell the fumes in the homes.

Let me ask if I can dance by the ocean. Let me see my memo.

Ask if they want tile in their villa or in their home.

al   all alert allow alone along ball fall hall salad shall usual

le   leg let lens legs lemon plea bless clean able hole mile tile

me   me met meet memo medal comes homes camera came come sometime

as   as ask asks aspirin base case cash easy task as has was seas

ll   allow bells bills hello sells villa all ill bell bill recall

ce   cell cent cedar cellar century faces scene ocean dance voice

Refer to page R-1 for tips on efficient keying of individual letters.

Timed Writings
(3'- and 5'-timed writings)

33. EMOTIONAL CONTROL

gwam 3'

	3'
In many cases, emotions involve strong feelings. Some peo-	4 | 50
ple have to make a special effort to control their emotions.	8 | 54
Lack of emotional control is sometimes observable on the job.	12 | 59
This lack of control is at times brought on by stress. Whatever	17 | 63
the reasons, a person should try to maintain control of emotions.	21 | 67
When emotions are out of control, a person frequently acts in a	25 | 72
way that is not acceptable to others. Lack of control may take	30 | 76
the form of complete withdrawal from ongoing activities or as an	34 | 80
outburst of outrage over some incident. A good rule is to remain	38 | 85
under emotional control at all times. In doing this, a person	43 | 89
serves as a role model for others who may have the problem.	46 | 93

gwam 3' | 1 | 2 | 3 | 4 |

34. PERSONAL QUALITIES

gwam 3' | 5'

	3'	5'
Personal qualities are important to you in about any kind	4	2 | 47
of situation that may occur. These qualities are often stated	8	5 | 50
in broad terms like personality, skills, values, and attitudes.	12	7 | 53
These kinds of qualities also are often stated in a broad way as	17	10 | 55
good or bad. For example, if you come to your job on time and	21	13 | 58
work hard you are described as a "good" worker. Good personal	25	15 | 60
qualities may occur without much conscious effort, while others	29	18 | 63
not as good may need much work to improve them. Bad ones that	34	20 | 65
you may find that you possess are the most difficult to change.	38	23 | 68
In a more narrow sense, personal qualities are often based	42	25 | 70
on how you feel about yourself. The self-image that you have of	46	28 | 73
yourself is regarded as your self-esteem or self-respect. Varied	51	30 | 75
studies often reveal that the higher your self-esteem, the more	55	33 | 78
likely you are to exhibit success on the job. If what you en-	59	35 | 80
vision of yourself is high, then you frequently expect more of	63	38 | 83
yourself. If you feel good about yourself, you may also feel	67	40 | 85
good about others. If you have doubts about any of your per-	71	43 | 88
sonal qualities, rethink how you feel about your self-image.	75	45 | 90

gwam 3' | 1 | 2 | 3 | 4 |
5' | 1 | 2 | 3 |

Session 8 — Skillbuilding

<table>
<tr>
<td>

8a ●

Conditioning Practice

Key each exercise at the right three times.

</td>
<td>

Alphabetic Practice

He apologized quickly even though he was just six minutes late for brunch.

Digraph Practice (ea ic il ne we pr ra)

eat teach area ice dice cubic ill wild pupil net toner fine west jewel owe pry apron raid braid era

</td>
</tr>
</table>

8b ● **E**

Evaluation ~ Analysis

Key the timed writing at the right.

Timed Writing

Before each person picks a career, he or she must know his or her own ability. He or she should then rate himself or herself often so that he or she then can practice each week to reach the next higher level. Each person should have his or her own career plan.

8c Individualized Practice

Key the drill according to the prompts on your screen.

8d WordChamp

Play the game WordChamp.

8e End of Class Procedure . . .

if you are not continuing to the next Session.

Speed Clinic

It was a nice idea. Did anyone see the new pupil? I raced.

After dinner take the camera to the opera. He was surprised that the nice music played on the weekends only.

ea   earn ease east easy earth deal dear earned pea tea area idea

ic   nice pick rice rich sick which basic logic music sonic topic

il   ill illegal illusion silk pencil mail sail pupil trail until

ne   new near neck news never knee dinner pine alone stone anyone

we   we wed wet weak wear were west owed power sweat sweet we owe

pr   pro prey prom press price pride print spray spread surprised

ra   ran race rack rail radios range brand era extra opera camera

Refer to page **R-1** for tips on efficient keying of individual letters.

31. PERSONNEL SELECTION

gwam 3'

When budgets of various firms are analyzed, one of the items	4	51
that requires the most expense is that of hiring personnel. Hir-	8	55
ing of new personnel is not only very costly, but is also time	13	59
consuming. The success or failure of a firm is often gauged by	17	64
how well its personnel are hired. Thus, a firm usually closely	21	68
examines the work experience and education of a job applicant be-	25	72
fore that person is hired. Work experience that relates direct-	30	76
ly to the job is often very helpful in the selective process. At	34	81
times, work experience not directly related to the job can help.	38	85
The formal education of a job applicant also influences the pro-	43	89
cess. An interview confirms if the applicant is the best choice.	47	94

gwam 3' | 1 | 2 | 3 | 4 |

32. MANAGING CONFLICTS

gwam 3' | 5'

Have you ever experienced a real conflict with a person? If	4	2	48
you have, this timed writing may take on special meaning for you.	9	5	50
If not, the day may come when such a conflict might occur. It	13	8	53
is often shocking how quickly a conflict can occur in a firm.	17	10	55
You need to show fairness in dealing with others to help prevent	21	13	58
conflicts. Conflicts between one employee and another employee	26	15	61
and at other times between an employee and an employer often	30	18	63
lower the level of production for a firm in which such conflicts	34	20	66
occur. A solution to a conflict may sometimes appear harsh.	38	23	68
To prevent or to control a conflict, you should try to pre-	42	25	70
vent or to slow down the conflict before it reaches a stage that	46	28	73
is difficult to correct. Obviously, the best solution is to pre-	51	30	76
vent the conflict. Thus, you must stay alert to the dynamics	55	33	78
that are taking place around you. Once you think a conflict is	59	35	81
going to occur, you and other persons may need to intervene imme-	63	38	83
diately. However, if a conflict has already occurred, this is	67	40	86
often more serious. In this case, you and other persons must	72	43	88
carefully evaluate the situation before trying to intervene.	76	45	91

gwam 3' | 1 | 2 | 3 | 4 |
5' | 1 | 2 | 3 |

Session 9 — Skillbuilding

9a •
Conditioning Practice
Key each exercise at the right three times.

Alphabetic Practice
Kent Brown just got five extra points on a computer quiz; he did very well.

Digraph Practice (hi be ro wi ec ta)
him ship hi bet abet cube roam wrong zero wins echo niece sec tax vitae data

9b • **E**
Evaluation ~ Analysis
Key the timed writing at the right.

Timed Writing
    If each person has his or her own career plan, each person can take control of his or her own future. Write a career plan that will lead to the job of your choice. Check your plan weekly. Don't be lazy. Success does not come quickly!

9c Individualized Practice
Key the drill according to the prompts on your screen.

9d WordChamp
Play the game WordChamp.

9e End of Class Procedure . . .
if you are not continuing to the next Session.

Speed Clinic

Maybe the wild bear is hidden near the highway. Do not be a hero. Be wise and swim to the wreck near the shore.

Please tag and label all the tan tables. Check the deck for wind damage. You can win a new wardrobe if you guess right.

hi hi him his high hire hidden highway chip ship this thinks hi

be be bee beg bear begin member liberty maybe describe wardrobe

ro row road rock roof room round drop proud wrote pro hero zero

wi win wide wife wild wind wise wish swim twin sewing worldwide

ec echo economy economic deck elect check decal decks wreck sec

ta tag tan tall tank table taste attack retail total data quota

Refer to page **R-1** for tips on efficient keying of individual letters.

29. HOW YOU EARN TRUST

gwam 3'

	3'	
Mostly, trust is a trait that is not quickly noted in a per- | 4 | 51
son. Trust is an example of a trait that is earned. To trust a | 8 | 55
person is to place reliance in the character, ability, or honesty | 13 | 60
of that person. Therefore, it is easier to trust persons who | 17 | 64
have demonstrated through varied actions that their trust is war- | 21 | 68
ranted. When you expect a person to trust you, the trust is also | 26 | 73
substantiated by your actions. The real test of trust is whether | 30 | 77
you or others have proven that trust is genuine and long lasting. | 34 | 82
As an employer, a primary responsibility is to ascertain whether | 39 | 86
others in a firm are trusted employees. To be successful, an em- | 43 | 90
ployee must purposely work in earning the trust of an employer. | 47 | 94

gwam 3' | 1 | 2 | 3 | 4 |

30. CONCERN AND LOYALTY

gwam 3' | 5'

	3'	5'
Another significant attitude affecting the workplace is that | 4 | 2 | 47
of concern. Too often there seems to be an adversarial relation- | 8 | 5 | 50
ship, rather than one of concern, between an employee and an em- | 13 | 8 | 52
ployer. Concern needs to be shown by both parties. One way an | 17 | 10 | 55
employer can show concern is to provide an employee with a good | 21 | 13 | 58
salary and good fringe benefits. Employees show concern for | 25 | 15 | 60
their employer by performing their jobs in a way that will help | 29 | 18 | 63
an employer meet the goals of a firm. Employees who do more than | 34 | 20 | 65
what is expected can expect to earn greater rewards. | 37 | 22 | 67

Loyalty is the employee trait that most shows concern for | 41 | 25 | 70
the employer, according to one survey. Loyalty comes into play | 45 | 27 | 72
when working out problems that are unpleasant in a firm. In | 50 | 30 | 75
other words, it is often very difficult to assess the loyalty of | 54 | 32 | 77
an employee until a critical incident arises in a firm. The | 58 | 35 | 80
character of a person is often shown by the loyalty that is dem- | 62 | 37 | 82
onstrated in this kind of incident. If an incident of this kind | 66 | 40 | 85
occurs in your firm, you must show your concern by doing your | 71 | 42 | 87
best to show loyalty to your employer by supporting its policies. | 75 | 45 | 90

gwam 3' | 1 | 2 | 3 | 4 |
     5' | 1 | 2 | 3 |

10a ●

Conditioning Practice

Key the exercise at the right three times.

Alphabetic Practices

Many judges will keep the size of bail equal to half the court expenses involved.

Wan was very quick to object; he realized the taxi fare might possibly be high.

He apologized quickly even though he was just six minutes late for brunch.

Kent Brown just got five extra points on a computer quiz; he did very well.

10b ● E

Evaluation ~ Progress

Key the first timed writing at the right.

10c ● E

Evaluation ~ Progress

Key the second timed writing at the right.

10d ●

WordChamp

Play the game WordChamp.

10e ●

End of Class Procedure . . .

if you are not continuing to the next Session.

Timed Writing

To be a good worker one must have not only the skills needed to perform a specific job, but also the desire to excel in that performance. Just realize that skill alone is not quite enough to do the job. Can you think of a job you had to do where skill alone was not good enough? Also ask others in your firm.

Timed Writing

A business is almost always judged by two factors: how good are the goods and services it provides and the people who work for it. Pick a business and see how it maximizes these two factors. Is it a large or small business? Does it provide a service, or does it sell a product? How many work for the business? Has it made a profit this past year? Can you think of any other questions you would ask?

Speed Clinic

Balanced-Hand Words

These are good word drills to key: panel, rhapsody, wobble, throttle, quake, pane, quench.

I blame Todd for the shape of shantytown. Angie may risk a pair of shamrocks.

pale pan panama pane panel quake quantify quell quench queen

rhapsody rib rich rid riddle rig right rigid rigor risk roam

shake shale shall sham shamble shame shamrock shanty soapbox

shantytown shape than the their them theme then theory they

throb throttle throw thrown ugh us usual usurp usury via vie

vigor virus visible whole wheel when wick widow wield wobble

27. FIRST IMPRESSION

gwam 3'

What do you think about the impression that a person makes	4 | 50
when you first meet him or her? Some persons think that the	8 | 54
first impression is the best way to determine what someone is	12 | 58
like. Think of some of your friends. Was this true of them? In	17 | 63
some instances, you were possibly accurate in analyzing someone	21 | 67
by a first impression. However, in most cases, you will find	25 | 71
that it takes more than the first meeting to discern what a per-	29 | 75
son is like. But the first impression may appear to give you	33 | 79
some idea, especially if a person exhibits negative qualities.	38 | 84
For example, you may observe poor speaking ability, improper	42 | 88
dress, and negative personal traits when you first meet a person.	46 | 92

gwam 3' | 1 | 2 | 3 | 4 |

28. BE A GENUINE PERSON

gwam 3' | 5'

Have you ever purchased a product that includes a guarantee	4 | 2 | 45
that it is genuine? Did you discover later that it was not genu-	8 | 5 | 48
ine? You were probably not happy with the product. You most	12 | 7 | 50
likely returned it for a refund. Unfortunately, dealing with	17 | 10 | 53
people who are not genuine is not as easy as dealing with a prod-	21 | 13 | 55
uct that is not genuine. One of the worst traits a person can	25 | 15 | 58
have is that of not being genuine. A person who isn't genuine is	29 | 18 | 61
insincere in both words and actions and may not be trustworthy.	34 | 20 | 63
How does a lack of genuineness hurt a firm? When firms work	38 | 23 | 66
with the outside world, they try hard to satisfy their custom-	42 | 25 | 68
ers. The same principle holds true for the working relations	46 | 28 | 71
among employees in a firm. If an employee is not genuine, this	50 | 30 | 73
may soon be recognized by other employees. Other employees may	55 | 33 | 76
resent an employee who is not sincere, and this will cause dis-	59 | 35 | 78
harmony in the firm. If the situation persists and affects your	63 | 38 | 81
work, you and others may wish to report it to the supervisor to	67 | 40 | 83
preserve quality customer service and the atmosphere of the firm.	72 | 43 | 86

gwam 3' | 1 | 2 | 3 | 4 |
          5' | 1 | 2 | 3 |

Session 11 — Skillbuilding

11a ●
Conditioning Practice

Key each exercise at the right three times.

Alphabetic Practice
Jack Bar realized that quality exercise was very important for good health.

Digraph Practice (si ch om pe et ca el)
sin visit chic yacht inch omit comma prom pea opera rope ethics diets let car vocal pica elm relax fuel

11b ● Ⓔ
Evaluation ~ Analysis

Key the timed writing at the right.

Timed Writing
   When you begin your first job in business, you will quickly see the value of what you have learned in school. Business persons expect you to come to work well prepared and expect you to be able to complete every task asked of you. Will you have the skill to be able to complete every task asked of you by your employer on the job? Will you succeed in your career?

11c Individualized Practice
Key the drill according to the prompts on your screen.

11d WordChamp
Play the game WordChamp.

11e End of Class Procedure . . .
if you are not continuing to the next Session.

Speed Clinic

Sit in the car and help sing a song. It was a size six top.

Get the anchor for the yacht. Come home to mom and your six room home. I hope the pet is well. Can you help elect him?

si sir sit six side sing size sincere basic music beside inside

ch chip chain chart cheap echo yacht anchor arch each inch much

om omit omits omission some atoms dome home come mom room broom

pe pen per pet peak peel pest peace open paper super hope shape

et ethics eternal ethical nets sets veto let met net pet forget

ca can cap car cat cake camp scale decade academy pecan replica

el elite fell help self well field else elect feel fuel flannel

Refer to page **R-1** for tips on efficient keying of individual letters.

25. TIMELINESS AT WORK

gwam 3'

Timeliness does not happen by chance, but rather is a result | 4 | 54
of good planning and organization. Do you plan and organize your | 9 | 59
time so that you appear promptly at meetings? If your answer is | 13 | 63
"no," you should keep an eye on the clock and leave for your | 17 | 67
meetings early. It is true that some foolish persons appear to | 21 | 71
pride themselves on being late to meetings. However, timeliness | 26 | 76
is a significant trait often fostered by employers. If an em- | 30 | 80
ployee is often late for work, earnings of an employer may be | 34 | 84
affected. Other employees are also often affected if an em- | 38 | 88
ployee is late. They may become upset because they have to do | 42 | 92
another's work. Again, if you have a tendency not to be on time, | 46 | 97
you should seize the opportunity to try to solve the problem. | 50 | 101

gwam 3' | 1 | 2 | 3 | 4 |

26. PATIENCE IS A VIRTUE

gwam 3' | 5'

A person who is capable of calmly awaiting a result or an | 4 | 2 | 47
outcome is patient. There appears to be a large variation in | 8 | 5 | 50
patience among employees. Your degree of patience may or may | 12 | 7 | 52
not be an asset to you on the job. Some employers, frequently | 16 | 10 | 55
in the field of selling, want people who show some impatience. | 21 | 12 | 57
The rationale is that persons who are considered too patient will | 25 | 15 | 60
not work as diligently toward meeting goals that may be set. | 29 | 18 | 62
Thus, the extent of patience needed to meet job demands varies, | 33 | 20 | 65
depending on the type of job and the type of people on the job. | 38 | 22 | 68

Most employers discourage the outward expression of im- | 41 | 25 | 70
patience. If you know that you are not being patient on a par- | 45 | 27 | 72
ticular day, try to control it in the same way that you control | 50 | 30 | 75
other factors that cause problems on your job. Try to conduct | 54 | 32 | 77
your work in a way that impatience does not have a direct effect | 58 | 35 | 80
on the job. Achieve balance by understanding that your impa- | 62 | 37 | 82
tience can cause you to do less than a perfect job. To exhibit | 67 | 40 | 85
control and balance with patience is a characteristic that will | 71 | 42 | 87
make your work and your workplace more pleasant and productive. | 75 | 45 | 90

gwam 3' | 1 | 2 | 3 | 4 |
5' | 1 | 2 | 3 |

12a ●
Conditioning Practice
Key each exercise at the right three times.

Alphabetic Practice
Hal was very quick to go criticize Jacob for the extra work placed on him.

Digraph Practice (ri ma li us nc ee)
rim trio may amaze aroma lie elite alkali use husky thus incur zinc eerie queen bee

12b ● **E**
Evaluation ~ Analysis
Key the timed writing at the right.

Timed Writing
Don't take a chance. Choose the right career for you, one that you will enjoy and that will make you happy. If you do not like your job, you can't expect to do your best work. If you are to realize your professional career goal, you must study hard in school.

12c Individualized Practice
Key the drill according to the prompts on your screen.

12d WordChamp
Play the game WordChamp.

12e End of Class Procedure . . .
if you are not continuing to the next Session.

Speed Clinic

Ride the raft to the rim of the river. I saw the image of a small animal. Look for the list in the library. The campus bus took us to the fancy dance. Mary fell from the tree and hurt her knee. I drank three cups of coffee at the concert.

Refer to page **R-1** for tips on efficient keying of individual letters.

ri | rim rice rich ride ribbons drink price write wrist potpourri

ma | man map maid mall math mark human format aroma comma diploma

li | lie lit lift like line lights clip slim policy public chili

us | us use used using busy house mouse bonus virus campus famous

nc | inch fence ounce ranch branch income pencil once launch zinc

ee | been deed deep feed keel meet need needs fee see free degree

23. EMPLOYEE RELATIONS

gwam 3'

Think of the great amount of time an individual spends on	4	51
the job during a lifetime. You will spend this time either as an	8	55
employee or an employer. Presently, you may or may not be in ei-	13	59
ther one of these roles. Whether you operate your own business	17	64
or work for someone else now or in the future, you will find that	21	68
the relations between an employee and an employer consume a great	26	73
amount of time. Regardless of whether you are an employee or an	30	77
employer, positive relations are needed. To make sure relations	34	81
are positive, an employer must always maintain fair treatment for	39	86
an employee. Similarly, an employee must realize early what is	43	90
required and follow through with the best relations possible.	47	94

gwam 3' | 1 | 2 | 3 | 4 |

24. SELECTING A CAREER

gwam 3' | 5'

How do you select a career that is right for you? You first	4	2	48
need to consider your aptitude and interest for certain careers.	8	5	51
You also need to study different careers. As you study, you will	13	8	53
find various types of sources useful to you. For example, ask	17	10	56
persons why they chose their careers. Try to learn if they are	21	13	58
satisfied or perhaps not satisfied with their choices. Learn	25	15	61
about careers from magazines, books, and pamphlets. Internet	30	18	63
sites with information about careers are helpful. The time you	34	20	66
spend in learning about careers is time that is well spent.	38	23	68
Once you reach a tentative career choice, reconsider what	42	25	71
aptitude and interest you may have in the selected career. When	46	28	73
you consider aptitude, try to discover if you have the ability to	50	30	76
learn and understand the skills and knowledge required in the se-	55	33	78
lected career. If you do not have a real interest in a career,	59	35	81
you most likely will be unhappy in it. Be careful not to select	63	38	84
a career that is short lived or gives very little opportunity for	68	41	86
changing to another career. Even with a good choice, a person is	72	43	89
still likely to change careers several times during a lifetime.	76	46	91

gwam 3' | 1 | 2 | 3 | 4 |
5' | 1 | 2 | 3 |

Session 13 — Skillbuilding

13a ●
Conditioning Practice
Key each exercise at the right three times.

Alphabetic Practice
Bev Mape quickly realized she was just ten cents short of the exact change.

Digraph Practice (ns ho ac ct di rs la)
tense vans hoe photo echo ace yacht almanac facts act dip edit first wars lab clad villa

13b ● Ⓔ
Evaluation ~ Analysis
Key the timed writing at the right.

Timed Writing
For many years some of the banks of this country have had financial problems. Most of these problems are the result of bad loans by banks. These banks did not follow the laws of their states. It is hoped that the next few years will see action taken to end the problem.

13c Individualized Practice
Key the drill according to the prompts on your screen.

13d WordChamp
Play the game WordChamp.

13e End of Class Procedure . . .
if you are not continuing to the next Session.

Speed Clinic

I lost a shoe at the shop. Please phone the media to check the name of the first victim. Answer the actor at the gala.

The doctor took fast action to save the victim.

ns sense tense answer insect insert cans fans lens pans transit

ho hog hop hot how hold hour honey shop shot show whom who echo

ac ace act acre actor accept action rack sack tact each almanac

ct facts action doctor victim active fact elect affect contract

di did dig dim dip dice dime dirt disc audio radio editor media

rs first horse marsh nurse purse cars ears hers jars ours stars

la lab lad lax lack lame lane lawn flag plan black gala manila

Refer to page R-1 for tips on efficient keying of individual letters.

21. TEAMWORK AND GOALS

gwam 3'

	3'
Sports events are often won as a result of teamwork. They	4	51
are often lost when there is a lack of teamwork. Working as a	8	55
team is very important in many situations. As a result of good	12	59
planning, most organizations have long- and short-term goals. In	17	64
most cases, each of the goals is easier to attain with a team ef-	21	68
fort. When hiring new employees, most organizations try to re-	25	72
cruit persons who will work as members of a team in sharing the	30	76
common goals that have been established. Persons are out of step	34	81
when their goals are inconsistent with those of the organization.	38	85
Although you need to develop your own goals, the goals of the	43	89
organization in which you are employed are also very significant.	47	94

gwam 3' | 1 | 2 | 3 | 4 |

22. MOTIVATION AT WORK

gwam 3' | 5'

	3'	5'
When a person is encouraged, that person is often strongly	4	2	48
motivated. One of the best kinds of encouragement is that which	8	5	50
ensues from intrinsic or internal motivation. When a person does	13	8	53
a good job, this often results in good feelings. For instance,	17	10	56
to complete a job that was not easy is often a form of encourage-	21	13	58
ment that is internal. A person is often encouraged by finishing	26	15	61
a routine job within less time than is expected. Thus, if a per-	30	18	63
son performs beyond what is expected in a job, the person may be	34	21	66
encouraged to proceed in doing an even better job next time.	38	23	68
Another method that is used to encourage a person is ex-	42	25	71
trinsic or external motivation. For instance, once a good job is	46	28	73
done, the person finishing the job is provided with one or more	51	30	76
tangible items for recognition. This type of motivation, which	55	33	78
is used often on the job, can take several forms. Raises and	59	35	81
awards are two examples. Mostly, these are given for job re-	63	38	83
lated purposes. Most experts often think that encouragement of	67	40	86
this kind is not as strong as that which is internal. Both kinds	72	43	88
of encouragement are likely to motivate a person on the job.	76	45	91

gwam 3' | 1 | 2 | 3 | 4 |
      5' | 1 | 2 | 3 |

Session 14—Skillbuilding

14a ●
Conditioning Practice
Key each exercise at the right three times.

Alphabetic Practice
Jake approached a very difficult extra job as equipment manager with zeal.

Digraph Practice (ss pl no rt ly pa)
asset boss plan people not know steno forty part lying flying rely page span spa

14b ● E
Evaluation ~ Analysis
Key the timed writing at the right.

Timed Writing
Place a portion of the money you earn each week in the bank. You will earn interest on the investments you place in the bank. The size of your investment will quickly increase at a just rate. Do not pass up the chance to have your money grow as it earns interest.

14c Individualized Practice
Key the drill according to the prompts on your screen.

14d WordChamp
Play the game WordChamp.

14e End of Class Procedure . . .
if you are not continuing to the next Session.

Speed Clinic

Refer to page **R-1** for tips on efficient keying of individual letters.

I would panic if I were a flyer in space. The artist starts soon on the northwest airpark. I noticed a light plane dive into the plaza. A witness issued a statement at the airport while the airport staff alerted the media.

ss   asset issue assign glossy lesson vessel boss less loss class

pl   plan plea plus plane plate plants apple couple simple supply

no   no nor not now none noon know snow canoe knot no piano steno

rt   birth carts earth north carton shirts parts hurts art report

ly   lying lynch flyers analyze only rely ugly apply daily family

pa   pan par pay pace paid park path repay space spark repair spa

19. PERSONALITY TRAITS

gwam 3'

Personality is the totality of the non-physical traits of a	4	50
person. Thus, personality is often reflected in the total of	8	54
good and bad traits of a person. In some people, these traits	12	58
tend to surface very quickly. In others, the traits are more	17	63
subtle and surface more slowly. Some tests can measure a per-	21	67
son's relative good and bad traits. However, how honest a person	25	71
is in answering questions on the tests will often have an effect	29	75
on how valid and reliable these tests are. Over a reasonable	33	79
period of time, the personality of a person can often be observed	38	84
with more meaning. However, how a person acts does not always	42	88
reveal much about how he or she really feels in a situation.	46	92

gwam 3' | 1 | 2 | 3 | 4 |

20. BUSINESS MANNERS

gwam 3' | 5'

In a business, a supervisor's manners toward an employee	4	2	47
depend on very simple rules of good etiquette. A friendly and	8	5	50
gracious attitude is a form of good etiquette. Such an attitude	12	7	53
can form the basis of a good working relationship. The kinds of	17	10	55
actions that a supervisor exhibits will likely be returned. As	21	13	58
the supervisor, it is up to you to demonstrate the kind of busi-	25	15	60
ness manners you wish employees to copy. This may not be easy,	29	18	63
but it often is a very rewarding experience. In the short and	34	20	65
the long run, good business manners will pay off for you.	37	22	68
Similarly, an employee's manners toward a supervisor also	41	25	70
depend on some simple rules of good etiquette. Listening very	46	27	72
closely to what is expected of you is a form of good manners. In	50	30	75
most instances, a supervisor expects you to work through proper	54	33	78
channels when dealing with persons on higher levels. This means	59	35	80
that your own supervisor is most often the first channel for	63	38	83
clearing your work, unless you have other instructions. A super-	67	40	85
visor expects you to always be on time and work hard. You are	71	43	88
then on your way to becoming a respected, well-liked employee.	75	45	90

gwam 3' | 1 | 2 | 3 | 4 |
5' | 1 | 2 | 3 |

15a ●
Conditioning Practice
Key the exercise at the right three times.

Alphabetic Practices

Jack Bar realized that quality exercise was very important for good health.

Hal was very quick to go criticize Jacob for the extra work placed on him.

Bev Mape quickly realized she was just ten cents short of the exact change.

Jake approached a very difficult extra job as equipment manager with zeal.

15b ● (E)
Evaluation ~ Progress
Key the first timed writing at the right.

15c ● (LA)
Evaluation ~ Progress
Key the second timed writing at the right.

15d ●
WordChamp
Play the game WordChamp.

15e ●
End of Class Procedure . . .
if you are not continuing to the next Session.

Timed Writing

In your search for job success, you must set your own personal goals as to what it is you wish to achieve. List and look at every one of your goals. Each must be practical in terms of your ability and your training. Keep in mind that every person is unique. Each has an idea of what it takes to be a success on the job. Do not be lazy. Do your very best to excel. In the end, you will have the feeling of having done your best.

Timed Writing

Establishing goals can help you to develop good work attitudes. This process can also lead to success on the job. Given the importance of good work attitudes, you will find that you will be much in demand. Once you have acquired a finalized list of goals, try to set short-term objectives. You can expand the list later to include long-term ones.

Speed Clinic

Balanced-Hand Words

The goal is to dismantle the dirigible. Di got a good gown.

I got the disk by the city chapel. The field hand got a man to keep the emblems. If the island is by the isle, then she might visit with a jeep or a bus.

am amble ambush amend amendment bit blame blanch bland blend

chaos chapel chaps city civic dirigible dish disk dismantle

elbow element elf emblems embody field hand field lens fiend

gib gig glair go goals good gory got gown ham hand handiwork

idle if iguana iris is island isle jay jeep jell keep kennel

lame lament land lane laps lapel laughs lay man manana mango

Timed Writings
(3'- and 5'-timed writings)

17. ORAL COMMUNICATIONS

gwam 3'

To orally communicate in an effective way is an asset to   4 | 50
you. To simply get a point across, you frequently need to talk   8 | 55
with others in a clear and concise manner. You may play a vital   12 | 59
role as telephone and video conference calls become more and   17 | 63
more common. Voice mail and answering machines will be used by   21 | 67
nearly everyone. In situations like these where your voice is   25 | 71
recorded, you must convey what you think in a kind and courteous   29 | 76
manner. If you ever use voice-activated input with the personal   34 | 80
computer, you will speak words rather than key them. Thus, you   38 | 84
should try to use good grammar at all times. You must also think   42 | 89
quickly so that you will always speak with meaningful content.   46 | 93

gwam 3' | 1 | 2 | 3 | 4 |

18. WORKING RELATIONS

gwam 3' | 5'

Good working relations do not happen by accident. To ensure   4 | 2 | 48
good working relations, it takes a great deal of effort. Can you   9 | 5 | 51
envision people with whom you need to relate well at your job?   13 | 8 | 53
As people often interact on the job, they must very firmly grasp   17 | 10 | 56
how to interact with others in varied groups. One group is com-   21 | 13 | 58
prised of employees. Another group is comprised of employers.   26 | 15 | 61
Also, people to whom a firm markets its goods and services is   30 | 18 | 63
another group with whom working relations occur. In all cases,   34 | 20 | 66
it is wise to possess good working relations with other people.   38 | 23 | 68

Once you comprehend what working relations are desirable in   42 | 25 | 71
firms, how do you maintain steady, positive working relations   46 | 28 | 73
with other people? First, you need to know yourself well enough   51 | 30 | 76
to overcome any negative feelings so that only positive feelings   55 | 33 | 78
affect your attitude on the job. Second, you need to perceive   59 | 36 | 81
that most other people are often trying to pursue a similar path   64 | 38 | 84
in having good relations on the job. Third, do not allow one   68 | 41 | 86
bad incident to keep you from taking an overall positive view to   72 | 43 | 89
seek good working relations with other people on the job.   76 | 45 | 91

gwam 3' | 1 | 2 | 3 | 4 |
       5' | 1 | 2 | 3 |

Session 16 — Skillbuilding

16a ●
Conditioning Practice
Key each exercise at the right three times.

Alphabetic Practice
Jacob May quickly realized he was required to pay a fee for every exchange.

Digraph Practice (fi ge po av os ad)
file define get agent page post export tempo avail gave oscillator cost autos admit made pad

---

16b ● Ⓔ
Evaluation ~ Analysis
Key the timed writing at the right.

Timed Writing
Going to the bank is a job Zelda does each day. She deposits all the money from sales and will have to request the change needed for the present day. The bank will then fax a receipt to her office. She views this task as a chance to advance in the business world.

16c Individualized Practice
Key the drill according to the prompts on your screen.

16d WordChamp
Play the game WordChamp.

16e End of Class Procedure . . .
if you are not continuing to the next Session.

Speed Clinic

The cadet got a badge and photos from the lady at no cost.

Upon leaving the airport we traveled to the caverns where we managed to use the huge bridge. He fixed my pole and caught fifty catfish. The naval officer gave a badge to me.

fi	fit fix file fill find firm fifth first define office profit
ge	get germ gets general agent angel agency edge huge page urge
po	pole poll pool poor port point sport coupon depot upon tempo
av	avoid avenue average aviator have save leave flavor favorite
os	cost loss lost rose autos cosmos memos photos radios asbestos
ad	add adds added adult address dads lads ad bad dad had spread

Refer to page R-1 for tips on efficient keying of individual letters.

15. SPECIAL DRILLS

Drill practice is a good way to help you with speed and con-	4 | 51
trol. To get the most out of your work, use the drills that may	8 | 55
help you with the most common types of problems. Finger and row	13 | 60
drills are very often used. You may need to work with the first,	17 | 64
second, third, and fourth fingers. You may also practice with	21 | 68
the first, second, third, and fourth rows. Work on the use of	25 | 72
the shift for capital letters is also needed. Work with double	30 | 77
letters and side-by-side letters, as these letters often cause	34 | 81
problems in words. When you key, spacing may be a major concern.	38 | 85
As you try to space in the right way, more drill practice in use	43 | 90
of the space bar may help. Work on what seems to help the most.	47 | 94

gwam 3' | 1 | 2 | 3 | 4 |

16. KEYING IN THE FUTURE

Most experts think that how we key in the future will	4 | 2 | 47
change little, if at all, from how we key now. Most anyone who	8 | 5 | 50
makes a study of the future will agree there will be new products	12 | 7 | 52
and changes in present ones that relate to keying. Even as these	17 | 10 | 55
changes take place, it seems that keying will not show a great	21 | 13 | 58
deal of change. Even with changes in different types of products	25 | 15 | 60
over the years, the place of the keys on a keyboard has had very	30 | 18 | 63
little change. This is the case even after studies show a heavy	34 | 20 | 65
load is on the left hand and the weaker fingers when one keys.	38 | 23 | 68
Have you thought about what is new now and how it will af-	42 | 25 | 70
fect those who key on the job or at home? More use of the Inter-	46 | 28 | 73
net will greatly affect how we do our work and have fun. When	50 | 30 | 75
you simply key an item in a search, the writings of experts can	55 | 33 | 78
be brought to you at work or home. Also, e-mail makes it as easy	59 | 35 | 81
to key a note to a friend far away as it is to a friend in a	63 | 38 | 83
local area. Even with voice input, keying will still be needed	67 | 40 | 86
to help edit copy. More use will be made of software that checks	72 | 43 | 88
your skill to key and helps you improve that skill.	75 | 45 | 90

gwam 3' | 1 | 2 | 3 | 4 |
      5' | 1 | 2 | 3 |

Session 17 — Skillbuilding

17a •

Conditioning Practice

Key each exercise at the right three times.

Alphabetic Practice

Kurt Bangor quickly realized the exact errors when he verified major plans.

Digraph Practice (ot ul lo em un su ai)

other vote not ultra full useful employ items them unit runs begun such insure aid bait

17b • **E**

Evaluation ~ Analysis

Key the timed writing at the right.

Timed Writing

Before Zelda goes to the bank, she adds all the money to make sure that no error was made. This takes a lot of time, about one hour per day. She usually does not find an error. To Paul her job seems easy. It is not until he sees how important it is that he quickly sees the responsibility that comes with her job. She is paid quite well for doing this task.

17c Individualized Practice

Key the drill according to the prompts on your screen.

17d WordChamp

Play the game WordChamp.

17e End of Class Procedure . . .

if you are not continuing to the next Session.

Speed Clinic

Refer to page **R-1** for tips on efficient keying of individual letters.

Haul the photo booth to the lower lobby. My aunt gave Uncle Otto an employee emblem. We cannot hunt for tuna in summer.

Go to the airport to get your aisle seat on the airline.

ot   other both note motor quota motel dot got hot pot knot pilot

ul   ulcer ultra ultimate bulk bull dull gulf hull haul wonderful

lo   low load loan lone look flow slow blond gallon hello buffalo

em   empty employ embassy memo enemy items tempo item seem system

un   uncle under unable united aunt fund hunt tune fun gun outrun

su   sum sun such suits sudden subway summer casual resume visual

ai   aim air aims aisle airline airport fail hail hair sail waist

13. TRANSPOSITION ERRORS

gwam 3'

A transposition error occurs when letters are not keyed in   4 | 52
proper position next to each other in a word.   This is one of the   8 | 56
most common types of errors that is made.   It may be hard to know   13 | 60
when this type of error is made as you key.   Some words are more   17 | 65
likely to cause this type of error.   For example, a word with two   22 | 69
letters next to each other that are keyed with the same fingers   26 | 73
on each hand may cause a problem.   These errors are often made in   30 | 78
short, easy words when the word patterns are not yet set well in   35 | 82
your technique.   Work this out by keying this type of word on the   39 | 86
letter level.   You should think of each letter of the word first;   43 | 91
then think of the whole word.   Use special drills, if they help.   48 | 95

gwam 3' | 1 | 2 | 3 | 4 |

14. KEYING MYTHS ON THE JOB

gwam 3' | 5'

Did you know a test given to check how fast a person keys   4 | 2 | 47
does not always show if that person is able to do well on the   8 | 5 | 50
job?   It is a myth to assume that how one keys on one or two   12 | 7 | 52
writings can reveal much about how one would key on the job as   16 | 10 | 55
a whole.   It has been found in studies about keying that the   20 | 12 | 57
skill to do good work on a writing under time does not correlate   25 | 15 | 60
to a great extent to how well various types of documents in a   29 | 17 | 62
firm are keyed.   Too many other factors, like work habits and ef- 33 | 20 | 65
ficiency, will affect the success of a person who keys on a job.   37 | 22 | 67

At times, you may key copy in which your fingers seem to   41 | 25 | 70
move with much ease.   At other times, your fingers may not seem   45 | 27 | 72
to want to work for you.   Do you think that you are not having a   50 | 30 | 75
good day when your fingers do not move as you wish?   That notion   54 | 32 | 78
is one more myth.   How hard the copy is can cause problems.   Copy 59 | 35 | 80
often ranges from an easy level to a much harder level.   The dif- 63 | 38 | 83
ficulty level of the copy can be often gauged by the types of   67 | 40 | 85
words in the copy.   Thus, you are most likely not having a good   71 | 43 | 88
or bad day; it may be the level of the copy you are keying.   75 | 45 | 90

gwam 3' | 1 | 2 | 3 | 4 |
       5' | 1 | 2 | 3 |

Session 18—Skillbuilding

18a ●
Conditioning Practice

Key each exercise at the right three times.

Alphabetic Practice
Jake Bittle made every effort to give Paul the exact answers for the quiz.

Digraph Practice (ut tr ts ow vi sh iv)
utmost cuts about try patrons itself arts own town visa advice she cashed rush ivory civil

18b ● E
Evaluation ~ Analysis

Key the timed writing at the right.

Timed Writing

When you need to pick a bank, you should shop around to find one that lets you earn a good rate of interest on your money. Five percent is a good rate. You should try to put part of the salary you earn each week into a savings account. Don't be lazy. Now is the time to start; you just can't wait. Place the maximum amount possible in a savings account each week. You will see that your money will quickly grow!

18c Individualized Practice
Key the drill according to the prompts on your screen.

18d WordChamp
Play the game WordChamp.

18e End of Class Procedure . . .
if you are not continuing to the next Session.

Speed Clinic

Try to take an auto on the country route. Who is the active owner of the fine ivory cows? Drive safely and stay alive.

Ship the vital virus in the five kits. I am very outspoken.

ut   utility utmost auto mouth route but out input layout without

tr   try tray tree trip trail trend extra country retreat streets

ts   acts arts bets cuts hats kits nuts outset footsteps nutshell

ow   owe owl own owns owner rows blows flows grows bow cow fellow

vi   via vim view virus vital victim evil civic civil movie civic

sh   she shy ship shop shall shape shelf dishes bushes ash polish

iv   ivy ivory five give live alive civic drive active ivy strive

Refer to page R-1 for tips on efficient keying of individual letters.

11. BASIC KEYING SKILLS

gwam 3'

Before you start any type of job where you use the keyboard,	4	51
you must build your keying skills to a proper level. One of the	8	56
most needed skills is the quick use of the enter key with steady	13	60
motion before, during, and after its use. A similar process is	17	64
needed for other special keys that are used very often. Examples	21	69
are the space bar, the tab key, and the shift. You also need to	26	73
learn the position of the letters and the proper finger to use	30	77
with each one of them. For success you should be able to easily	34	81
key short words, phrases, and sentences. Also, you should try to	39	86
keep in mind the whole process for proper keying that you have	43	90
learned as you do your work every day at school and on the job.	47	94

gwam 3' | 1 | 2 | 3 | 4 |

12. KEYING MYTHS IN CLASS

gwam 3' | 5'

To learn how to key the right way, practice is the answer.	4	2	49
This is a myth unless you learn to do the right kind of practice.	9	5	51
Practice with purpose and meaning is needed to key the right way.	13	8	54
A story has been told about a class in which all of the students	17	10	57
were able to key far above the speed and control level that was	22	13	59
expected by the end of the first school term. During this time,	26	16	62
the class only worked with timed writings on the letter keys.	30	18	64
This is a very sad story. The extent of the content was too	34	21	67
narrow and the practice did not have real purpose and meaning.	39	23	69
When you learn to key, watch out for myths that might keep	43	26	72
you from working in the best way. For instance, when you try to	47	28	74
develop the skill to key, you do not work on speed and control at	51	31	77
the very same time. You often need to move from your best speed	56	33	80
level to a slower speed level at which you can have the best con-	60	36	82
trol. It will confuse you if you try to attain your best speed	64	38	85
and control at the same time. While it is often good to compete	68	41	87
in sports, it is a myth that competing with others improves key-	73	44	90
ing speed or control. Compete only against yourself when keying.	77	46	92

gwam 3' | 1 | 2 | 3 | 4 |
5' | 1 | 2 | 3 |

Session 19—Skillbuilding

19a ●
Conditioning Practice

Key each exercise at the right three times.

Alphabetic Practice

Bart G. Quincy just won a six-week Rome holiday vacation as first prize.

Digraph Practice (so wh ie ni op ld)

sold lesson also who nowhere diet movie nice united alumni open copy stop holds old

19b ● (E)
Evaluation ~ Analysis

Key the timed writing at the right.

Timed Writing

Do not expect anyone else to plan for your future. View "saving" as the means to secure your future. Plan for a stable future; know that you have money in the bank that is earning the highest possible rate of interest. Don't stop saving. Put a little money in the bank each week while you are young so that you will have a lot of money in the bank when you are older.

19c Individualized Practice

Key the drill according to the prompts on your screen.

19d WordChamp

Play the game WordChamp.

19e End of Class Procedure . . .

if you are not continuing to the next Session.

Speed Clinic

Who what why and when are good questions. Junior and I went to see a whale movie last night. It was a cold season at my resort. It was cold on opening night at the opera.

so   so son sow soap sock soda soft sold south absorb resort also

wh   who why what when whom whale wheel who somewhere everywhere

ie   diet lies pier tier view alien brief fried lie pie tie movie

ni   nice nine niece night ninth nickel knit junior tennis alumni

op   open opera opener option opening opposite copy hope top drop

ld   holds older builds colder golden old bald bold cold gold old

Refer to page R-1 for tips on efficient keying of individual letters.

9. YOUR COMFORT LEVEL

gwam 3'

The comfort level for keyboarding lies between the levels	4 | 50
of speed and control. For example, if you work at a rate that	8 | 55
is between your fastest speed and one that gives the most con-	12 | 59
trol, you are at your comfort level. This is the rate with	16 | 63
which you should key your regular work, not the rate you use when	21 | 67
keying a timed writing or drill to build your speed and control.	25 | 71
Thus, it is the level at which you have a feeling of ease--you	29 | 76
are not forced to key too fast for speed or too slow for control.	34 | 80
When you work at this level, you do not feel stress that might	38 | 84
relate to speed or control. The result is steady, even keying.	42 | 89
If a good product is your goal, try to key at the comfort level.	46 | 93

gwam 3' | 1 | 2 | 3 | 4 |

10. KEYING AND THE MOUSE

gwam 3' | 5'

When you key at the computer, you will work with the mouse,	4	2 | 48
an input device. Its shape is not always the same. It has more	8	5 | 51
than one button, but you will mainly use the left button. If you	13	8 | 53
use your left hand, it can be changed so that you may use the	17	10 | 56
right button. After working with the mouse, you know that the	21	13 | 58
main process is to point at a place on the monitor and then click	26	15 | 61
one or two times to get the results that are needed. The rate	30	18 | 64
with which the mouse will point and click can be adjusted. Some	34	20 | 66
of the file items you can point to include open, save, and close.	38	23 | 69
Now that you know something about the mouse and its use, how	42	25 | 71
do you work with it? At first you may feel that you cannot con-	47	28 | 74
trol the mouse. With practice it is as easy as pointing your	51	30 | 76
finger. You also need to learn to keep the mouse in the center	55	33 | 79
of your mouse pad and to point and click quickly. You must be	59	36 | 81
able to point quickly to a place that you select on the monitor.	64	38 | 84
Once you point to the place that is correct, you are ready to use	68	41 | 87
the button. You then need to click one or two times. In either	72	43 | 89
case, press and let go of the button at a very fast rate.	76	46 | 91

gwam 3' | 1 | 2 | 3 | 4 |
5' | 1 | 2 | 3 |

20a •

Conditioning Practice

Key the exercise at the right three times.

Alphabetic Practices

Jacob May quickly realized he was required to pay a fee for every exchange.

Kurt Bangor quickly realized the exact errors when he verified major plans.

Jake Bittle made every effort to give Paul the exact answers for the quiz.

Bart G. Quincy just won a six-week Rome holiday vacation as first prize.

20b • **LA**

Evaluation ~ Progress

Key the first timed writing at the right.

20c • **LA**

Evaluation ~ Progress

Key the second timed writing at the right.

20d •

WordChamp

Play the game WordChamp.

20e •

End of Class Procedure . . .

if you are not continuing to the next Session.

Balanced-Hand Words

Timed Writing

The purpose of an interview is to get data and to give data. It is probably one of the most important tasks you will have to do in obtaining a job. The employer must be favorably impressed to hire you. You must organize your facts so that you can give the exact data requested in the fastest time possible. What does the employer need to know about you?

Timed Writing

Accounting records give us an historical background of an enterprise from its very beginning. Certain records are required to be on file at all times. They can be examined routinely by investigators. You just need to know which need to be kept. Would you like to take a course in accounting? There are dozens of texts which can help you if you wish to learn. Plan to be prepared.

An ancient burial box held a box and bowl. I am the mentor.

I am a buckeye. It is an enamel emblem. Both fish may die.

She lent me the keys to their neighbor's dog kennel. May I pay for the endowment by the end of the visit?

an ancient and angle ant bogus born borne both bottle burial

bow bowl box clams clamshell clan clang clap clemency clench

clay cool clement dismay disorient disown dispel divisor end

enamel enchantment endow endowment endue fig fight fir firms

figment fish glen gurney guru gush hut guzzle hairy he ivory

irk it ivy kept keys lay down lend lens lent mane may mentor

7. BUILDING SPEED

gwam 3'

Speed will vary less than control over time. In other | 4 | 50
words, speed is often stable from day to day while control is | 8 | 54
not. Thus, you can see gains in speed easier than you can gains | 12 | 58
in control. To build speed with good form in your work, you must | 17 | 63
have good posture, build proper control of keys, concentrate on | 21 | 67
your work, use the fingers in a proper way, and keep your eyes on | 25 | 71
the copy. These are not all of the ways to help build speed-- | 29 | 76
only some of the best ones. You need to move very fast with | 33 | 80
various types of keying drills to help build speed, but not at | 38 | 84
the expense of doing away with proper techniques. If you try to | 42 | 88
increase speed to very high levels, you often decrease control. | 46 | 92

gwam 3' | 1 | 2 | 3 | 4 |

8. COPY, CUT, AND PASTE

gwam 3' | 5'

	3'	5'
To copy and cut text is a simple process when you use word | 4 | 2 | 48
processing software. When the copy process is used, the words | 8 | 5 | 50
that you copy will stay in the same place while they also are | 12 | 7 | 53
moved to some other place in the copy. You may cut words in much | 17 | 10 | 55
the same way. Once you cut words, they no longer remain where | 21 | 13 | 58
they were, but may be pasted in another spot in your document or | 25 | 15 | 60
removed. To copy words that you want to use in another place in | 30 | 18 | 63
the document, you first highlight them. Then move the cursor to | 34 | 20 | 66
the place where you want the copy and use the copy command. | 38 | 23 | 68
As you can copy and cut words within one document, you can | 42 | 25 | 70
also paste words to other documents. To do this, a storage area | 46 | 28 | 73
that is often known as the Clipboard is used. When you move | 50 | 30 | 75
words from one place to some other place, they will first be | 54 | 33 | 78
placed in the storage area. Your computer will do this on its | 58 | 35 | 80
own--you do not need to use a new command. When you paste words, | 63 | 38 | 83
you remove them from storage and insert them where you have | 67 | 40 | 85
placed your cursor. Keep in mind that when you cut or copy you | 71 | 43 | 88
are pasting words that were stored for a time on your Clipboard. | 75 | 45 | 90

gwam 3' | 1 | 2 | 3 | 4 |
5' | 1 | 2 | 3 |

Session 21—Skillbuilding

21a ●
Conditioning Practice
Key each exercise at the right three times.

Alphabetic Practice
Kurt Ford was amazed by just missing the very same exit as Quincy P. Long.

Digraph Practice (ci mo ol ay bl)
city decide most among memo old golf cool mayor away black table

21b ● **E**
Evaluation ~ Analysis
Key the timed writing at the right.

Timed Writing
Jack must go to the bank each day and deposit the following: checks, paper money, and coins. He did not like to go to the bank very much when it was cold, but he realized this daily business transaction was part of his job. He did like the exercise he was able to get when he walked to the bank.

21c Individualized Practice
Key the drill according to the prompts on your screen.

21d WordChamp
Play the game WordChamp.

21e End of Class Procedure . . .
if you are not continuing to the next Session.

Speed Clinic

He is famous for modern dancing. The oldest mayor got a big diamond. The memo said to spray the pool. She sold most of her blue blankets to the blacksmith. Is her hair black or a light blond? My birthday is on a holiday this year.

Let's take a trip down the oldest waterway in the city soon.

ci   city civic civil circle cities citizen decide social stencil

mo   mom mop mow mood moon more smoke almost remote memorize memo

ol   old older olive oldest folk hold poll sold told cool control

ay   pays says ways maybe mayor payee rayon bay day hay lay delay

bl   blow blue black blade blond blood able cable noble ably able

Refer to page **R-1** for tips on efficient keying of individual letters.

5. COPY DIFFICULTY

gwam 3'

	3'
Copy is often rated on how hard it is to key by the length | 4 | 51 |
of the words, the number of syllables, and the number of words | 8 | 55 |
from a list of common words. When all three of these factors are | 13 | 59 |
present at a set level, you have what is known as triple-control | 17 | 64 |
copy. How hard the copy is has an effect on the results that you | 21 | 68 |
may have with speed or control. For instance, the writing that | 26 | 72 |
you are keying right now is rated as easy, which is the lowest | 30 | 76 |
level. If you compare your work on this writing with another | 34 | 81 |
writing, make sure that the other writing is rated as easy. If | 38 | 85 |
you compare your speed on writings from different levels, they | 42 | 89 |
will not make sense. So note the level before you key a writing. | 47 | 93 |

gwam 3' | 1 | 2 | 3 | 4 |

6. KEYING ENVELOPES

gwam 3' | 5'

If you key letters in a firm, you often deal with both mail | 4 | 2 | 48 |
coming in and going out. For mail coming in, you must open the | 8 | 5 | 50 |
envelope, remove the contents, check and account for items that | 13 | 8 | 53 |
may be enclosed, stamp the time of receipt, and often send the | 17 | 10 | 55 |
envelope and its contents to some other place in the firm. If | 21 | 13 | 58 |
you work with mail that is going out, you need to know the postal | 25 | 15 | 60 |
rules. A copy of an up-to-date postal guide will help you with | 30 | 18 | 63 |
this process. Even if you work in a large firm that has a cen- | 34 | 20 | 65 |
tral place to handle mail, it is still good to know the rules. | 38 | 23 | 68 |

If you use a word processor that lets you key an envelope, | 42 | 25 | 70 |
it is very easy to address. The one to whom a letter is sent is | 46 | 28 | 73 |
the same address that is copied on the front of the envelope. If | 51 | 30 | 76 |
your firm does not have its own address on the envelope, it is | 55 | 33 | 78 |
easy for you to have one ready to copy. Thus, you may make and | 59 | 35 | 81 |
keep a copy of any address for mail going out or coming in for | 63 | 38 | 83 |
future use. You can add the envelope to the file where the out- | 67 | 40 | 86 |
going letter is placed. It is very easy to change the format | 72 | 43 | 88 |
of the envelope so that you may use the most common sizes. | 75 | 45 | 90 |

gwam 3' | 1 | 2 | 3 | 4 |
5' | 1 | 2 | 3 |

Session 22—Skillbuilding

22a ●
Conditioning Practice
Key each exercise at the right three times.

Alphabetic Practice
Jack said that next year's budget size for equipment was very equal.

Digraph Practice (na ir mp mi im rd tt am)
name final arena iris hire their ample ramp mind smile imply time claim order word attend watt among fame cam

22b ● **E**
Evaluation ~ Analysis
Key the timed writing at the right.

Timed Writing
Quincy had to get each deposit slip in order for Jack each day. Most of the time that he used to complete this important job came in the morning. He also had to sign his name on the deposit slip. He would then circle the amount of the deposit so that no errors would be made. He is committed to doing a good job.

22c Individualized Practice
Key the drill according to the prompts on your screen.

22d WordChamp
Play the game WordChamp.

22e End of Class Procedure . . .
if you are not continuing to the next Session.

Speed Clinic

Do you like the name Nancy for a girl? I like Betty. I admit the camp was empty. Mix the cards for Steven and him.

na name navy names nation snap canal banana arena china antenna

ir iron bird dirt fire firm girl tire wire air fir sir fair air

mp ample empty lamps ramps tempo campus ample empty tempo camps

mi mix mild mile milk mill mind mine mink omit admit submit mix

im import imagine aims dime time climb limit aim dim him victim

rd birds cards cords lords order border bird card record reward

tt attic ditto petty watt attach attack putty watt boycott watt

am am amend among ample amount came camp fame lame same am team

Refer to page R-1 for tips on efficient keying of individual letters.

3. HOW TO SET TABS

gwam 3'

The tab is used often at the start of a paragraph. When	4 | 50
software is used to key copy, a default tab stop is most likely	8 | 55
to be set at every half inch. You can set a stop at any place on	13 | 59
the page. The process to set a stop is not hard. It is easy and	17 | 64
quick to move to a stop by pressing the tab key. You may also	21 | 68
need to move a stop or delete or create one or more new ones.	25 | 72
This, too, is an easy and quick process. Think of the time that	30 | 76
you can save when you use tabs with tables that have more than	34 | 80
one column. Tabs are moved less in letters because of the in-	38 | 85
crease in use of the block style. In block letters you start all	42 | 89
parts of the letter at the left margin or at the first left stop.	47 | 93

gwam 3' | 1 | 2 | 3 | 4 |

4. KEYING REPORTS

gwam 3' | 5'

A report is one of the most common types of documents. If	4	2 | 48
you are new to a firm in which reports are often keyed, you will	8	5 | 50
need to know what format is used for the reports of the firm.	13	8 | 53
The reports will often range from simple in-house reports to very	17	10 | 56
complex reports. A firm in which reports are keyed on a routine	21	13 | 58
basis will often have a manual to use as a guide. The manual	25	15 | 61
will often have rules for margins, spacing, and other items	29	18 | 63
needed to key a report for the firm. In case the firm does not	34	20 | 66
have a manual, the use of file copies of reports should help.	38	23 | 68
There are some rules for keying reports that are common to	42	25 | 70
most firms. Most reports start with a title that is centered at	46	28 | 73
the start of a report. The first page of a report often does not	50	30 | 76
have a page number. You cannot divide a word at the end of a	55	33 | 78
page. It is often a rule that at least two lines must be in a	59	35 | 81
paragraph at the bottom of a page. When it is possible, the	63	38 | 83
same rule is in effect for lines on the next page of a report.	67	40 | 86
Often, long quotes of four or more lines are indented in the body	71	43 | 88
of a report. Reports for a firm may be either bound or unbound.	76	45 | 91

gwam 3' | 1 | 2 | 3 | 4 |
     5' | 1 | 2 | 3 |

Session 23 — Skillbuilding

23a ●
Conditioning Practice
Key each exercise at the right three times.

Alphabetic Practice
George quickly adjusted the taxi fare when quizzed by a very mad person.

Digraph Practice (wa ab wo id pp oo ep)
was away about cable cab work sworn idea wide did upper book too pep epoxy kept step

23b ● E
Evaluation ~ Analysis
Key the timed writing at the right.

Timed Writing

While she was about to go into the bank where she worked each day, Nancy did not watch her step and slipped on the floor. Within only a few minutes, her arm quickly felt like it had been broken. She asked to leave work early so she could have it checked. After an X-ray was taken, she was told that her arm would feel better within a few days.

23c Individualized Practice
Key the drill according to the prompts on your screen.

23d WordChamp
Play the game WordChamp.

23e End of Class Procedure . . .
if you are not continuing to the next Session.

Speed Clinic

Always wait to walk. The label was missing on the wool baby cot. Ideally kids can ride with approval. Keep the book on the porch steps. Get a worker to do the cable paperwork.

wa   was wax way wait walk wall want warm away await awake always

ab   able about above absent baby tabs cable label cab lab prefab

wo   wood wool word work words sworn worker artwork paperwork two

id   idea idle ideal ideas ideally kids lids ride side aid liquid

pp   apples poppy appeal copper apply upper happy approve support

oo   book cook foot hook pool room took books doors floor shampoo

ep   epidemic episode kept depot depth steps accept deep keep pep

Refer to page R-1 for tips on efficient keying of individual letters.

Timed Writings
(3'- and 5'-timed writings)

1. KEYING FOR CONTROL

gwam 3'

If you want a final copy that does not have an error, keying	4 | 51
for control is very important. To key for control means to key	8 | 55
at a rate that is easy for you to manage for both speed and accu-	13 | 59
racy. As you key, you must be in focus to make sure that you are	17 | 64
always under control. To stay under control, you may need to	21 | 68
slow down your rate of speed for a higher level of control. Try	26 | 72
to key words and phrases rather than letter by letter. Always	30 | 76
keep your eyes on the copy and be sure to use good technique with	34 | 81
your fingers at the keyboard. Some control is not enough; you	38 | 85
must have full control at all times. If you have problems with	43 | 89
control, do more practice with the goal of control in mind.	47 | 93

gwam 3' | 1 | 2 | 3 | 4 |

2. NUMBER/SYMBOL KEYS

gwam 3' | 5'

The numbers or figures on the top part of a keyboard are not	4 | 2 | 48
easy to learn. One of the reasons is that you spent a lot of	8 | 5 | 50
time at first with the letter rows, which do seem easier. The	12 | 7 | 53
letter rows are easier since they are either on or next to the	17 | 10 | 55
home keys. Also, the numbers or figures seem harder because they	21 | 13 | 58
are not used over and over again in a sentence. However, these	25 | 15 | 61
numbers or figures should become much easier to key as you prac-	30 | 18 | 63
tice them more and more. There are some drills you can do that	34 | 20 | 66
will help you learn to key the numbers and figures with ease.	38 | 23 | 68
The symbols are often thought to be the most difficult of	42 | 25 | 70
all the keys, including the number or figure keys. Almost all of	46 | 28 | 73
the symbols are on the same keys as the numbers or figures and	50 | 30 | 76
must be used with the shift key, which may help explain why they	55 | 33 | 78
are so difficult. In any case, you must not expect to key the	59 | 35 | 81
symbols as fast as letters. As with numbers or figures, the sym-	63 | 38 | 83
bols will become easier to key with practice if this is a goal	67 | 40 | 86
you have. If you work on a job that requires you to key symbols	72 | 43 | 88
over and over again, you will learn to use them very quickly.	76 | 45 | 91

gwam 3' | 1 | 2 | 3 | 4 |
5' | 1 | 2 | 3 |

Session 24 — Skillbuilding

24a ●

Conditioning Practice

Key each exercise at the right three times.

Alphabetic Practice

Kim Forbes said the grand prize quoted was adjusted to include every tax.

Digraph Practice (ry tu ia if ap fe)

rye trying jury tube actual trial media if gift apart tapes map felt offer safe

24b ● **E**

Evaluation ~ Analysis

Key the timed writing at the right.

Timed Writing

Until Nancy knew her arm was not broken, she just continued to worry. Once she was told that her arm would feel better, she returned to work within a few minutes. She did not want to appear lazy. Her boss told her to take the remainder of the day off and/or if she wanted to stay at work, to go to the employee lounge until the end of the workday. She did not want to receive special treatment.

24c Individualized Practice

Key the drill according to the prompts on your screen.

24d WordChamp

Play the game WordChamp.

24e End of Class Procedure . . .

if you are not continuing to the next Session.

Speed Clinic

When you return from the bakery you can study. I got a gift for my wife. What is your golf handicap? I prefer a cup of coffee. The amiable aviator has pneumonia. Check for a map in the encyclopedia. Hurry with the media story.

Refer to page **R-1** for tips on efficient keying of individual letters.

ry   rye dryer crying frying dry pry try jury vary very angry dry

tu   tub tube tune turn tulip turns tunnel stub setup stuck stuff

ia   giants pianos trial aerial diaper giants via media cafeteria

if   if gift rife drift gifts rifle life fifth knife lift wife if

ap   apple apart apply apiece appeal appear maps tape cap gap lap

fe   fed few fee fear feed feet feel fees offer coffee life knife

125a ●
Conditioning Practice
Key the exercise at the right three times.

Alphabetic Practices

Vic and Kim will expect the quarterly golf magazine by the end of July.

Locate these streets for me: Ixora, Grouper, Hawaii, York, Zircon, Venus, Queen, Jardin, Bunker.

Les gave Libby a diamond. Zack sent six pieced quilts for their June wedding.

Victor realized relaxed technique was to be a major key for quality typing.

125b ● A
Evaluation ~ Progress
Key the first timed writing at the right.

125c ● A
Evaluation ~ Progress
Key the second timed writing at the right.

125d ●
WordChamp
Play the game WordChamp.

125e ●
End of Class Procedure . . .
if you are not continuing to the next Session.

Speed Clinic

Timed Writing

One of the modern tools available to you in preparing your business reports is the computer. The computer performs all your mathematical figuring and provides a record of its computations in the form of printouts. The computer is a very unique tool. It is not a luxury but a necessity in our modern business world. It will help you to keep your records organized. After you become familiar with it, you will wonder how you did the job without it.

Timed Writing

Listening is so important that business is paying for good listeners. The person who does not listen is, in fact, a waster. Here are some of the situations under which listening takes place: we listen to a customer, an employer, or just a friend. We also listen to machines. What kinds of machines are involved? How frequently do you listen to them? Approximately how much time do you listen to machines? Would you like to minimize the amount of time you spend listening to them?

Planning on taking a vacation? If so, where? Yes, it's fun to plan a vacation. Go to a travel agent or read the travel brochures. How much time do you have for your vacation? We suggest you do your planning early. Give yourself plenty of time to plan. Go to the library and get references on where you wish to travel.

Will you need a passport? What about a physical examination? Also, be prepared to plan on what to do about your responsibilities at home.

Your employer needs to be notified. If you have a pet at home you will need to see that the pet is properly cared for. Have a happy time!

Session 25 — Assessment

25a ●
Conditioning Practice

Key the exercise at the right three times.

Alphabetic Practices

Kurt Ford was amazed by just missing the very same exit as Quincy P. Long.

Jack said that next year's budget size for equipment was very equal.

George quickly adjusted the taxi fare when quizzed by a very mad person.

Kim Forbes said the grand prize quoted was adjusted to include every tax.

25b ● LA
Evaluation ~ Progress

Key the first timed writing at the right.

Timed Writing

Be sure to keep your paragraphs short and to the point. Many of us will generally shy away from reading a long paragraph. Equally so, we will avoid reading text that appears to be a maze of words. Let the major topics stand out clearly. Make the text short and clear. A good rule to follow is to write for the reader. Try this activity. Write a short letter. Then write a long letter.

25c ● LA
Evaluation ~ Progress

Key the second timed writing at the right.

25d ●
WordChamp

Play the game WordChamp.

25e ●
End of Class Procedure . . .

if you are not continuing to the next Session.

Timed Writing

Punctuality on the job is imperative. It demands that you arrive at the office on time and that you complete your work on time. You must be on the job on time and be able to work to your maximum throughout the day. In order to accomplish this, you need to start planning and organizing the day before. Plan to acquire this important trait early in your career.

Balanced-Hand Words

Is the robot by the rock? Visit the tidy antique shelf. Vi is the sick visitor. Offhand I wish the owl, the dog, and the cow had a visitor.

Pay the visitor for the audit work. The ape is very sick.

neigh neighbor neurosis offhand official or orient ornament

pansy pant papa papal papaya pay rituals roan rob robot rock

shapen she shelf shell shriek shrub shrug sick thru tibia us

tic tick tidy tie tight tissue visit visitor visor visual ye

vivid weld wig wiggle wiry wish wisp wit with work yak yang

yap ye yell zig antique ape apricot apt audible audit burlap

Session 124 — Skillbuilding

124a ●
Conditioning Practice
Key each exercise at the right three times.

Alphabetic Practice
Victor realized relaxed technique was to be a major key for quality typing.

Symbols Practice (< > :)
k<k <k< k<k <k< l>l >l> l>l > <l> :;: ;:; ;:; :;:

124b ● **D**
Evaluation ~ Analysis
Key the timed writing at the right.

Timed Writing
Everyone in the classroom was amazed at just how limited were the true logical abilities of any computer. Only three logical operations are needed to allow the computer to perform thousands of tasks at very fast speeds. The three logical operations: equal to, =, greater than, >, and less than, <, allow many people to use all kinds of popular computer applications software, such as word processing, databases, and spreadsheets.

124c Individualized Practice
Key the drill according to the prompts on your screen.

124d WordChamp
Play the game WordChamp.

124e End of Class Procedure . . .
if you are not continuing to the next Session.

Speed Clinic

Symbols

> Refer to pages **R-2-R-3** for tips on efficient keying of individual symbols.

The sign on the door read: WordChamp Game Room. This symbol > means greater than. This symbol < means less than.

The months of the meetings are these: May, October, and November.

k< k< k< k< k< k<k k<k k<k k<k k<k k< k<k k< k<k k< k<k k< <

l> l> l> l> l> l>l l>l l>l l>l l>l l> l>l l> l>l l> l>l l> >

k<>l k<>l k<>l k<>l k<>l <k>l <kl> <kl> <kl> <kl> k<>l k<>l

<milk> <mill> <million> <minimum> <mom> <moon> <my> <kimono>

:;: :;: :;: :;: :;: :;: :;: :;: :;: :;: :;: :;: :;: :;: :;:

26a ●
Conditioning Practice
Key each exercise at the right three times.

Alphabetic Practice
Pam Jacob very quickly realized it was difficult to find the tax gain.

Digraph Practice (ag ty sa bo ex uc cl)
ago wage flag type style saw resale mesa boy about jumbo exit next index much class cycle

26b ● LA
Evaluation ~ Analysis
Key the timed writing at the right.

Timed Writing
Many graduates face the mammoth task of finding a first office job. Many people say that the average person will be employed in a new job about seven different times during one lifetime. You should not expect to obtain a good job by luck. It is clear that you should strive to develop your ability to a very high level to obtain and keep a good position.

26c Individualized Practice
Key the drill according to the prompts on your screen.

26d WordChamp
Play the game WordChamp.

26e End of Class Procedure . . .
if you are not continuing to the next Session.

Speed Clinic

Rachel has an empty handbag. Can somebody type these pages?

Jeffrey set sail on the same boat that Nicholas was on. Uncle Bob was unclear about the next clue. Stacey was very lucky.

ag   age ago again agent bags page wage image bag tag zag handbag

ty   type typing typist style teletype city duty dirty empty city

sa   say sat safe said sail sale same sang usage resale mesa visa

bo   boy box boat body bold bond about above ebony somebody jumbo

ex   excel extra exist excuse export next text texts sex textbook

uc   duck luck much such lucky touch truck bucket lettuce voucher

cl   club clue clad claim clip class uncle circle decline nuclear

Refer to page **R-1** for tips on efficient keying of individual letters.

123a
Conditioning Practice
Key each exercise at the right three times.

Alphabetic Practice
Les gave Libby a diamond. Zack sent six pieced quilts for their June wedding.

Symbols Practice (< > ? !)
k<k <k< k<k <k< l>l >l> l>l >l> ;? ?;? ;?; ?;? aq1! !1qa q1!a 1!qa

123b • D
Evaluation ~ Analysis
Key the timed writing at the right.

Timed Writing

Ophelia Unitas just asked her computer literacy class this puzzling question: "How many logical operations can a computer perform?" Natalie believed the answer was seven! Rebecca believed the answer was over one hundred! Steven was very excited because he believed that the precise answer was three. Steven was correct! A computer can determine if one number is equal to another number, =; greater than another number, >; or less than another number, <.

123c Individualized Practice
Key the drill according to the prompts on your screen.

123d WordChamp
Play the game WordChamp.

123e End of Class Procedure . . .
if you are not continuing to the next Session.

Speed Clinic

Symbols

Nicholas won the big game! One is < two. Eleven is > ten.

How old will you be on April 10? Did Lester win the case?

k< k< k< k< k< k<k k<k k<k k<k k<k k< k<k k< k<k k< k<k k< <

l> l> l> l> l> l>l l>l l>l l>l l>l l> l>l l> l>l l> l>l l> >

k<>l k<>l k<>l k<>l k<>l <k>l <kl> <kl> <kl> <kl> k<>l k<>l

<milk> <mill> <million> <minimum> <mom> <moon> <my> <kimono>

Yes! Charge it now! Look out! Stay awake! Don't drive!

Should I meet Bob at 8 a.m.? Or is 10 a.m. better for you?

This symbol > means greater than. This symbol < means less than. The symbol <> is used in many computer applications.

Refer to pages R-2-R-3 for tips on efficient keying of individual symbols.

27a ●
Conditioning Practice
Key each exercise at the right three times.

Alphabetic Practice
Kimberly Paul found the size quoted was just over the exact legal limit.

Digraph Practice (ev ke qu bu ov ig)
even seven key asked like quiz equal bus album oven move igloo high big

---

27b ● LA
Evaluation ~ Analysis
Key the timed writing at the right.

Timed Writing

You must remember that in business your work will be evaluated both on its quality and quantity. If you want to excel, you must keep busy and complete all work assigned to you to the best of your ability so that none must be done over. You can't just assume that your job will be there forever. You will be rewarded for the zeal with which you strive to complete your daily work.

27c Individualized Practice
Key the drill according to the prompts on your screen.

27d WordChamp
Play the game WordChamp.

27e End of Class Procedure . . .
if you are not continuing to the next Session.

Speed Clinic

Every evening the lake level rose. It was quite a quiz. He was overpaid but kept busy until eight. How did they manage to get done by seven? The ambulance squad left the suburbs.

Please ignore the light in the oven. Where is my keyboard?

ev ever evil event every evening fever level never seven eleven

ke key keen keep kept keys keyboard asked lakes rekey fake cake

qu query quiet quite quick quiz equip squad equal square unique

bu buy burn busy buys bust bulb album suburb tabulate ambulance

ov ovens overt over overdue overrun love move above cover glove

ig ignore ignorance high sign eight fight light big dig jig pig

Refer to page R-1 for tips on efficient keying of individual letters.

122a ●
Conditioning Practice
Key each exercise at the right three times.

Alphabetic Practice
Locate these streets for me: Ixora, Grouper, Hawaii, York, Zircon, Venus, Queen, Jardin, Bunker.

Symbols Practice ({ })
;{ {;{ ;{; {;{ ;}; }; }; }; ;{; {;{ ;{; {;{ ;}; }; }; }}

122b ● D
Evaluation ~ Analysis
Key the timed writing at the right.

Timed Writing

Mr. Zerelli instructed Elisa to always insert a space before the left brace symbol, {, but never after it, and to always insert a space after the right brace symbol, }, but never before it! Elisa certainly didn't believe that she would have very many opportunities to utilize the brackets or the braces in her writing. Mr. Zerelli informed Elisa that she would have many opportunities to utilize both brackets, [], and braces, {}, as she continued writing in her more advanced journalism courses.

122c Individualized Practice
Key the drill according to the prompts on your screen.

122d WordChamp
Play the game WordChamp.

122e End of Class Procedure . . .
if you are not continuing to the next Session.

Speed Clinic

Symbols

Journalism majors will no doubt encounter the symbol {} in their classes. This symbol {} is very useful to them.

;{ ;{ ;{ ;{ ;{ ;{; ;{; ;{; ;{; ;{; ;{; ;{; ;{; ;{; ;{; ;{;

;} ;} ;} ;} ;}; ;}; ;}; ;}; ;}; ;}; ;}; ;}; ;}; ;}; ;};

;{}; ;{}; ;{}; ;{}; ;{}; ;{}; ;{}; ;{}; ;{}; ;{}; ;{}; ;{};

Use this symbol {} to enclose a set in arithmetic. Try it.

This symbol {} can be useful when you want to use braces.

{auto} {jazz} {baseball} {football} {basketball} {soccer}

The new car can cost her several thousand dollars {$18,750}.

My fee {$100} is all I charge. Their fee {$150} is higher.

Refer to pages R-2-R-3 for tips on efficient keying of individual symbols.

28a ●
Conditioning Practice
Key each exercise at the right three times.

Alphabetic Practice
Ben Freed was very quick to realize that good luck must just plain exist.

Digraph Practice (gr du rm ff ny sp)
grade agree duty adult farms term offer bluff nylon anyway many spa aspen crisp

28b ● LA
Evaluation ~ Analysis
Key the timed writing at the right.

Timed Writing
As a new employee, you agree to perform specific duties for agreed upon wages. One of the first things any new employer will want to know is the skills you have that make you the person for the job. Many office jobs, today, will require that you have some experience using a computer.

28c Individualized Practice
Key the drill according to the prompts on your screen.

28d WordChamp
Play the game WordChamp.

28e End of Class Procedure . . .
if you are not continuing to the next Session.

Speed Clinic

Refer to page **R-1** for tips on efficient keying of individual letters.

Jeff needs an adult aspirin. The farmer wears dungarees. I need a uniform for the kickoff. Leave the canyon before the dust storm. Can anyone grow green grass? My newspaper said the suspect was a grocer. Take a tablespoon with you.

gr   grew grade grand grow grass grip agree angry diagram degrees

du   due dug dual duck duke dull duty ducks dummy adult educators

rm   army farms firms forms terms farmer formal arm farm warm arm

ff   offer affair affect afford coffee differ off cuff puff staff

ny   nylon nylons anyway anyone any tiny deny many agony symphony

sp   spa span spot spur space spare speak speed aspen crisp grasp

Session 121 — Skillbuilding

121a ●
Conditioning Practice
Key each exercise at the right three times.

Alphabetic Practice
Vic and Kim will expect the quarterly golf magazine by the end of July.

Symbols Practice ({ })
;{ {;{ ;{; {;{ ;}; };} ;}; };} ;{; {;{ ;{; {;{ ;}; };} ;}; };}

121b ● D
Evaluation ~ Analysis
Key the timed writing at the right.

Timed Writing

In her writing, Elisa Aquilina knew when she needed to apply brackets, []; however, she did not always know when she needed to use braces, {}. Her journalism instructor, Enrico Zerelli, explained that braces, {}, are usually used to enclose figures, a set in arithmetic, staffs in musical notation, and/or to enclose words.

121c Individualized Practice
Key the drill according to the prompts on your screen.

121d WordChamp
Play the game WordChamp.

121e End of Class Procedure . . .
if you are not continuing to the next Session.

Speed Clinic

Symbols

Using this symbol {} in your computer work is important. I suggest you study the options requiring the use of the {}.

;{ ;{ ;{ ;{ ;{ ;{ ;{ ;{ ;{ ;{ ;{ ;{ ;{ ;{ ;{

;} ;} ;} ;} ;} ;}; ;}; ;}; ;}; ;}; ;}; ;}; ;}; ;}; ;};

;{}; ;{}; ;{}; ;{}; ;{}; ;{}; ;{}; ;{}; ;{}; ;{}; ;{}; ;{};

Use this symbol {} to enclose a set in arithmetic. Try it.

This symbol {} can be useful when you want to use braces.

{auto} {jazz} {baseball} {football} {basketball} {soccer}

The new car can cost her several thousand dollars {$18,750}.

My fee {$100} is all I charge. Their fee {$150} is higher.

Refer to pages R-2-R-3 for tips on efficient keying of individual symbols.

Session 29—Skillbuilding

29a ●
Conditioning Practice

Key each exercise at the right three times.

Alphabetic Practice

Zelda Van bought the necklace as a gift for just six equal weekly payments.

Digraph Practice (do ei ef fr od da ue)

does random outdo eight being effect left belief from defray odd body food day adapt agenda guest true

29b ● LA
Evaluation ~ Analysis

Key the timed writing at the right.

Timed Writing

One of the major issues considered by an employer will be your ability to operate a computer to do the tasks that might be asked of you. Once you begin working, you will see the benefit of the training you have received in school. The effort you put forth on the job today will pay major dividends in the future. Don't be afraid; pursue your career with zeal!

29c Individualized Practice

Key the drill according to the prompts on your screen.

29d WordChamp

Play the game WordChamp.

29e End of Class Procedure . . .

if you are not continuing to the next Session.

Speed Clinic

Dad and mom went to the barbecue and dance with their chief.

I want a soda from the dairy. My neighbor asked a vendor if they could see the receipts. I bought fresh fruit from him.

do   do dot dock does doll done dog do odors meadow outdo tornado

ei   eight eighth eighty eighteen heir being seize their neighbor

ef   effort effects efforts efficient left theft before left beef

fr   free from frank fresh fruits afraid refrain confront infrared

od   odd odds odors body soda goods foods rod sod food good flood

da   dad dam day damp dark data adapt daytime dancers soda agenda

ue   fuel blues cruel query guests due sue blue clue glue overdue

Refer to page R-1 for tips on efficient keying of individual letters.

Session 120—Assessment

120a ●
Conditioning Practice
Key the exercise at the right three times.

Alphabetic Practices

Angela completed six crossword puzzles in five hours. Yes, I can bike with Jill this quarter.

The judge questioned Quincy yesterday. Frank and Pam left an extra brown velvet coat at the zoo.

Hal will eventually qualify for jury duty. Six bikers came to the big pizza party.

Jack asked Vic Quinlin to define these computer terms: byte, bug, syntax. Will can from A to Z.

120b ● A
Evaluation ~ Progress
Key the first timed writing at the right.

120c ● A
Evaluation ~ Progress
Key the second timed writing at the right.

120d ●
WordChamp
Play the game WordChamp.

120e ●
End of Class Procedure . . .
if you are not continuing to the next Session.

Speed Clinic

Timed Writing

It is usually accepted that there are seven key elements that lead to effective written communications. The written data has to be attractive, courteous, accurate, concise, complete, clear, and simple. Examine some of the letters you receive. Analyze the data to see if all the seven elements are included. Just in case you need to refer to a good letter, plan to quickly build a file of good letters for future use.

Timed Writing

When your boss conducts a review of your job performance, there are many aspects he or she needs to consider, such as the volume and quality of your work. Also examined are how you organize your work, carry out your assignments, and communicate information. Finally, there are the personal qualities such as maturity, cooperation, attitude, and motivation. All of these form a blend leading to a portrait of you as a worker. How well do you measure up? What are your weaknesses? And what are your strengths?

The computer will be your new working tool. It is important that you learn computers and the skills needed to use them efficiently. You should have had a course in computer literacy. What about a course in computer applications? Yes, this course is needed.

Some applications are these: spreadsheets, databases, and, of course, word processing. Also, there are graphic programs and drafting programs. Try to become knowledgeable with all of these software programs. Also learn the operating system of your computer. Learning to use a computer is not hard.

The computer is a tool and as such requires patience to use.

30a ●
Conditioning Practice
Key the exercise at the right three times.

Alphabetic Practices

Pam Jacob very quickly realized it was difficult to find the tax gain.

Kimberly Paul found the size quoted was just over the exact legal limit.

Ben Freed was very quick to realize that good luck must just plain exist.

Zelda Van bought the necklace as a gift for just six equal weekly payments.

30b ● LA
Evaluation ~ Progress
Key the first timed writing at the right.

30c ● LA
Evaluation ~ Progress
Key the second timed writing at the right.

30d ●
WordChamp
Play the game WordChamp.

30e ●
End of Class Procedure . . .
if you are not continuing to the next Session.

Speed Clinic

Balanced-Hand Words

Timed Writing

Throughout most of our history, nearly all data was sent orally. Today much of our business is being done through the means of credit. We have begun to emphasize more and more the importance of written communications. Just note the amount of data being sent by fax. Most firms and government agencies all require that data be kept in some type of written form. What kinds of data are kept by your company? And for how long? Does it send faxes?

Timed Writing

Many of us wish to have our own business. If you did have your own, what kinds of problems would you encounter? Can you guess? Are the problems unique to your business? Try to zero in on those areas you expect to cause problems. Just as an example, perhaps the business venture has the problem of where and how to obtain funds to establish facilities necessary to operate. Have you encountered this problem? How did you solve it?

The auditor is a burley buckeye. She is an ensign. Use the bugle to do dixieland and gospel. Fix the fishbowl handles.

He is the cashier for the bus corps. Did Bud bury the dog?

I got a map of the coalfield. The pens are a memento also.

auditor auditory aught buck buckeye bud bug burley coalfield

bugle burn burp bury bus cob chair cockeye cocoa cod corps

divot dixieland do dock doe dog dogie enrich ensign ensue do

fishbowl fit fix fizz flair flak gosh gospel handle handy he

mantis mantel maps me meld melt memento men mend meow pelvis

pelt pelvic pens penal penalty rod rogue rosy rot rotor ruby

Session 119—Skillbuilding

119a ●
Conditioning Practice
Key each exercise at the right three times.

Alphabetic Practice
Jack asked Vic Quinlin to define these computer terms: byte, bug, syntax. Will can from A to Z.

Symbols Practice ([ ])
;[; [;[;[; [;[;];];] ;];];] ;[; [;[;[; [;[;];];] ;];];]

119b ● **D**
Evaluation ~ Analysis
Key the timed writing at the right.

Timed Writing

The plus symbol usually indicates addition in most programming languages. Xaviera knew that the plus symbol is used to indicate mathematical addition; she didn't know the virgule, /, usually indicates mathematical division. The brackets, [], are used to correct mistakes in a verbatim quote and/or to indicate the writer's or another's comments within a quotation. Xaviera was told to space before the left bracket, [, but not after it; and to space after the right bracket,], but not before it.

119c Individualized Practice
Key the drill according to the prompts on your screen.

119d WordChamp
Play the game WordChamp.

119e End of Class Procedure . . .
if you are not continuing to the next Session.

Speed Clinic

Symbols

Refer to pages **R-2–R-3** for tips on efficient keying of individual symbols.

We will need to correct all errors [all] in the text. Can't they obtain them [all records] from the computer disks also?

;[;[;[;[;[;[; ;[; ;[; ;[; ;[; ;[; ;[; ;[; ;[; ;[; ;[; [

;] ;] ;] ;] ;] ;]; ;]; ;]; ;]; ;]; ;]; ;]; ;]; ;]; ;]; ;];]

;[]; ;[]; ;[]; ;[]; ;[]; ;[ ]; ;[ ]; ;[ ]; ;[ ]; ;[ ]; ;[ ];

[use] [this] [symbol] [to] [make] [comments] [in your text].

Let's sing "Happy Birthday" [all together] to Angela now.

Look for the left and right bracket [] on your keyboard.

Use the proper technique when typing the left bracket [.

Use the proper technique when typing the right bracket].

31a ●
Conditioning Practice
Key each exercise at the right three times.

Alphabetic Practice
Quickly jot down the exact size voltage for buying a washing machine part.

Digraph Practice (gh cu ck up oc ew ua)
ghettos eight laugh cut focus backs luck upon super group occur lock havoc ewes new dual

31b ● LA
Evaluation ~ Analysis
Key the timed writing at the right.

Timed Writing
Just a quick review of want ads for business office positions shows that you can earn a high income in exciting business offices. However, it might not have occurred to you, but most pupils do not learn to key while going to school. Being able to key has a dual purpose; it is valuable in the business office and in everyday life.

31c Individualized Practice
Key the drill according to the prompts on your screen.

31d WordChamp
Play the game WordChamp.

31e End of Class Procedure . . .
if you are not continuing to the next Session.

Speed Clinic

The crew flew eight missions last night. They were lucky.

The ocean upset the couple. The documents weigh a ton and could upset the couple. It lacks an even quart of oil.

gh	ghettos eight fight light might night right high laugh weigh
cu	cup cut cube cuff curb cure cuts curbs acute focus documents
ck	decks jacks lacks locks lucky back buck deck neck pack black
up	up upon upset couple pupil super occupy up cup group checkup
oc	occur ocean occupy occurs occupied dock lock rock sock havoc
ew	ewes few new sew blew crew drew flew grew knew new interview
ua	dual equal guard quart squad annual casual equal dual actual

Refer to page R-1 for tips on efficient keying of individual letters.

118a ●
Conditioning Practice
Key each exercise at the right three times.

Alphabetic Practice

Hal will eventually qualify for jury duty. Six bikers came to the big pizza party.

Symbol Practice (/)

;/; /;/ ;/; /;/ ;/; /;/ ;/; /;/ ;/; /;/ ;/; /;/ ;/; /;/ ;/; /;/

118b ● (D)
Evaluation ~ Analysis
Key the timed writing at the right.

Timed Writing

Xaviera Kirby was keying a computer program when she realized she kept making the mistake of keying a \ for a /. The symbol / is called the diagonal, the slash, or occasionally, the virgule. Xaviera didn't know that she could always use the diagonal, /, between two words to indicate that the meaning of either word pertains; i.e., and/or. In addition, the slash could be used as a dividing line in dates or fractions; i.e., 4/23/94 or 1/6. The virgule, /, is also used as the division symbol in almost all programming languages and in particular mathematical applications.

118c Individualized Practice
Key the drill according to the prompts on your screen.

118d WordChamp
Play the game WordChamp.

118e End of Class Procedure . . .
if you are not continuing to the next Session.

Speed Clinic

Symbols

The diagonal can be used as either a dividing line or as a division symbol. 6/19/34 or 6/17/39. 400/4=100; 4/2=2.

;/; ;/; ;/; ;/; ;/; ;/; ;/; ;/; ;/; ;/; ;/; ;/; ;/;

;//; ;//; ;//; ;//; ;//; ;//; ;//; ;//; ;//; ;//; ;//; ;//;

pop/ mop/ pup/ mop/ pop/ mop/ pop/ mop/ pop/ mop/ pup/ mop/

soap;/ soap;/ soap;/ soap;/ soap;/ soul;/ soul;/ soul;/

This symbol / is on your keyboard. Type this symbol: /////.

Type this on your screen: cut/ paste/ edit/ print/ save/.

The / symbol is very useful in working your programs. Okay!

Katelyn tried to find the / symbol on her keyboard as well.

Refer to pages R-2–R-3 for tips on efficient keying of individual symbols.

Session 32—Skillbuilding

32a ●

Conditioning Practice

Key each exercise at the right three times.

Alphabetic Practice

Eva Baker couldn't find time to enjoy the prizes for winning the tax quiz.

Digraph Practice (rn by fu fa ga ip)

earns turn bylaw baby's hereby fun refund fair befall alfalfa gas legal pipe clip

---

32b ● **LA**

Evaluation ~ Analysis

Key the timed writing at the right.

Timed Writing

Unless you are lazy, by the time you have completed school, you will have already invested many hours into your future. You will then be ready to face the business world because what you have learned in school will help you gain the courage to wipe out most of the competition.

32c Individualized Practice

Key the drill according to the prompts on your screen.

32d WordChamp

Play the game WordChamp.

32e End of Class Procedure . . .

if you are not continuing to the next Session.

Speed Clinic

If the barn burns the corn will be lost. The gala affair is to be held in the fall. The baggage is in the lobby. Those golf grips are for the game. The fall affair was fun and we had a wonderful time. The new luggage was a bargain.

rn burns earns turns barn born burn corn earn horn turn eastern

by by bylaw bypass baby's by baby ruby hobby lobby hereby baby

fu fun fur fuel full fund fuse fuss fully awful joyful powerful

fa fad fan far fat face fact fall affair befall default alfalfa

ga gal gap gas gay gage gain gala game gang again began baggage

ip pipe ripe tips wipe grips pips dip hip lip tip zip chip dip

Refer to page **R-1** for tips on efficient keying of individual letters.

Session 117 — Skillbuilding

117a ●
Conditioning Practice
Key each exercise at the right three times.

Alphabetic Practice
The judge questioned Quincy yesterday. Frank and Pam left an extra brown velvet coat at the zoo.

Symbols Practice (- = ')
;-; -;- ;-; -;- ;=; =;= ;=; =;= ;-; -;- ;-; -;- ;=; =;= ;=; =;= ;'; ';' ;'; ';'

117b ● Ⓓ
Evaluation ~ Analysis
Key the timed writing at the right.

Timed Writing
Wesley's professor also told him that he should use one hyphen, -, when dividing a word; however, he should use two hyphens, --, to indicate a dash. In addition, no space should precede or follow the dash. Another problem Wesley's professor noticed was that Wesley was using the equal sign, =, in sentences. He suggested that Wesley confine the use of the equal sign, =, to explicitly mathematical calculations and formulas.

117c Individualized Practice
Key the drill according to the prompts on your screen.

117d WordChamp
Play the game WordChamp.

117e End of Class Procedure . . .
if you are not continuing to the next Session.

Speed Clinic

Symbols

This symbol - is the hyphen. It's used as a punctuation mark.

This symbol = is the equal sign. It's used in math formulas.

p- ;- ;- ;p- ;p- ;p- ;p-; ;p-; ;p-; p- p- p- p- ;-; ;-; ;-;

p= p= p= ;p= ;p= ;p= ;p=p= ;p=p; ;p=p; p= p= p= p= ;p=; ;=;

;' ;' ;' ;'; ;'; ;'; ;'; ;' ;' ;' ;' ;' ;' ;' ;'; ;' ;';

-=' -=' -=' -=' -=' -=' -=' -=' -=' -=' -=' -=' -=' -=' -='

Use one hyphen - to divide a word: af-ter, a-gain.

Look at this formula (6-4=2). Another 8-4=4. A-B=C, 1-0=1.

don't can't won't I'll I've isn't Dad's Mom's Marney's Tom's

Don't call at Ted's home. The answer is 4-0=4. It's okay.

Refer to pages R-2-R-3 for tips on efficient keying of individual symbols.

33a ●
Conditioning Practice
Key each exercise at the right three times.

Alphabetic Practice

The exact size of Bradley's fee proved quite high just to make a new will.

Digraph Practice (gi ui eg cr ak ba)

begin forgive suit egg legal beg create acre makes speak bank debate

33b ● LA
Evaluation ~ Analysis
Key the timed writing at the right.

Timed Writing

Many people who work in urban business offices do not take the time each morning to have a good breakfast. You should take the time each morning to begin your day with juice, an egg, toast, cereal with cream, and milk. Give your business day a very good start; follow this very important practice each day.

33c Individualized Practice
Key the drill according to the prompts on your screen.

33d WordChamp
Play the game WordChamp.

33e End of Class Procedure . . .
if you are not continuing to the next Session.

Speed Clinic

With his makeup he was mistaken for Nicholas. Did she begin the craft quiz? My bakery made cakes for the football game.

Let's do eggnog for the college debate. My bathroom is back by the bar. Who built those college buildings?

gi begin logic magic rigid begins engine margin origin register

ui quit quiz suit build built equip fluid fruit guide buildings

eg egg eggnog began begin begins begun college telegram leg beg

cr crack craft cradle crafts crane acre across aircraft recruit

ak baked bakery brake cakes makes streaks peak sneak speak weak

ba baby back bag bald bale bar combat debate football bathrooms

Refer to page **R-I** for tips on efficient keying of individual letters.

Session 116 — Skillbuilding

116a ●
Conditioning Practice
Key each exercise at the right three times.

Alphabetic Practice
Angela completed six crossword puzzles in five hours. Yes, I can bike with Jill this quarter.

Symbols Practice (_ " ,)
;_; _;_ ;_; _;_ ;_; _;_ ;_; _;_ ;"; ";" ;"; ;"; ";" ;"; k,k ,k, k,k ,k, k,k

116b ● Ⓓ
Evaluation ~ Analysis
Key the timed writing at the right.

Timed Writing

Wesley Zaccheus was preparing a critical research paper for his sophomore journalism class. He wasn't entirely certain whether to place a book title in quotation marks, ", or whether to underline, _, the title. His journalism professor, Violet Quincy, advised Wesley that the title of every journal article should appear in quotation marks, ", and the title of every book should be underlined, _.

116c Individualized Practice
Key the drill according to the prompts on your screen.

116d WordChamp
Play the game WordChamp.

116e End of Class Procedure . . .
if you are not continuing to the next Session.

Speed Clinic

Symbols

"Do not begin to key," Rachel warned "until you hear Jeffrey say the word." Names of books should be underlined, _.

;_ ;_ ;_ ;p_ ;p_ p_ p_ p_ p_ ;_ ;p_ ;p_ ;p_ ;p_ ;p_ ;_ ;_ ;_

;" ;" ;" ;" ;" ;" ;" ;" ;" ;" ;" ;" ;" ;" ;" ;" ;" ;" ;"

k, k, k, k,k k,k k,k k,k k,k k,k k,k k,k k,k k,k k,k k,k k,k k,k

,"_,"_,"_,"_,"_,"_,"_,"_,"_,"_,"_,"_,"_,"_

kick, kick" kick_ kick, kick" kick_ kick, kick" kick_ kick,

Use this symbol _ to underline words that need underlining.

This symbol " represents quotation marks. A right and left.

This symbol , is called a comma. Use it in your writing.

> **Refer to pages R-2-R-3 for tips on efficient keying of individual symbols.**

Session 34—Skillbuilding

34a •
Conditioning Practice
Key each exercise at the right three times.

Alphabetic Practice
Kevin was able to enjoy quick recognition for realizing his maximum speed.

Digraph Practice (ye ls va ds um sc pi)
yes buyer dye also calls vary advance friendships lands umpire jumped gum scan fiscal disc pica typist

34b • LA
Evaluation ~ Analysis
Key the timed writing at the right.

Timed Writing

Yes, it is very important that every business person begin every morning with good food. Discuss your food with an expert, and pick a variety of food. If the food you like fails to meet your needs, be very quick to make a change in your diet. Summarize what you eat, and choose your food very carefully.

34c Individualized Practice
Key the drill according to the prompts on your screen.

34d WordChamp
Play the game WordChamp.

34e End of Class Procedure . . .
if you are not continuing to the next Session.

Speed Clinic

The scholars ordered pizzas. The lawyer and the taxpayer do not have the same opinions. The pupils used school pencils. Titanium golf clubs are popular. Landscape the vast yards.

Refer to page **R-1** for tips on efficient keying of individual letters.

ye   yes yet yeah year years dyed eyes players lawyer rye dye eye

ls   also else false pulse oils balls bells bills deals baseballs

va   van vans vary vast vague valid naval canvas savage advantage

ds   landscape hardship friendship words yards trends tends deeds

um   umbilical jump jumbo humor humid gums sums titanium momentum

sc   scale scan scars scene scent scope subscribe transcribe disc

pi   pivot pizza pits pine pier apiece alpine typing typist topic

115a ●
Conditioning Practice
Key the exercise at the right three times.

Alphabetic Practices

Hank and Zack won the most tournaments last year except for Bill. I was quick to judge the victory.

I bought a PC with a modem, fax, and monitor for their zoo. In seven years Jake will quit.

Can Wendy name six of the great books? Shirley found a pair of size seven quality jeans.

Kyle is a scuba diver. How many fathoms can Bridget dive? I plan to jump with Enzo, Tex, and Quinn.

115b ● Ⓐ
Evaluation ~ Progress
Key the first timed writing at the right.

115c ● Ⓐ
Evaluation ~ Progress
Key the second timed writing at the right.

115d ●
WordChamp
Play the game WordChamp.

115e ●
End of Class Procedure . . .
if you are not continuing to the next Session.

Speed Clinic

Timed Writing

Communication can be defined as the exchange of information and ideas. This exchange may be either oral or written. The origin of oral exchanges is as old as history itself. Throughout most of our history, almost all knowledge was transmitted through the spoken word. Today, just as in the past, oral exchanges are very important. How do we learn oral skills? Have you ever had an oral quiz in school?

Timed Writing

Modern civilization has refined and extended its physical environment so that we now have a much wider range in which to communicate orally. Today we are able to use a great amount of electronic equipment that is meant to help us communicate orally. With such devices, we are able to communicate over vast distances with people worldwide. Just think of the advances that can be made in the next century.

If you are not ready for college at this time, you should be thinking of getting a job that has job advancement for you. Talk to your friends. Read the want ads in your newspaper.

Set up an interview as soon as you find a suitable job. But be prepared! Know about the company. Know the appropriate dress required. And practice some of the interview steps.

Chances are you will begin at what is known as entry level. Do you know what questions to ask? What is the pay level? Will you be paid by the hour or will you be on salary? When you have answers to these questions you will be on your way.

Session 35—Assessment

35a ●
Conditioning Practice
Key the exercise at the right three times.

Alphabetic Practices

Quickly jot down the exact size voltage for buying a washing machine part.

Eva Baker couldn't find time to enjoy the prizes for winning the tax quiz.

The exact size of Bradley's fee proved quite high just to make a new will.

Kevin was able to enjoy quick recognition for realizing his maximum speed.

35b ●
Evaluation ~ Progress
Key the first timed writing at the right.

35c ●
Evaluation ~ Progress
Key the second timed writing at the right.

35d ●
WordChamp
Play the game WordChamp.

35e ●
End of Class Procedure . . .
if you are not continuing to the next Session.

Timed Writing

Keep in mind that no matter how small a business is, standard accounting practices can be applied to it. It may be your job to acquire the skills needed to become somewhat of an expert in how to keep these records. They must be comparable to those of your local, state, and federal government and must be accurate not only in math operations but also in accounting practices. Take the time to analyze what you will need to know.

Timed Writing

A knowledge of accounting is important both to the worker and to the company in making economic choices. Yes, certain principles must be known. What are some you will be expected to know? Jot these choices down. Do not worry about the size of your list. Inquire from a fellow worker as to what is important. Also you may want to ask why the items are important. Finally, you will need to verify your list with the one made by your fellow worker.

Speed Clinic

Balanced-Hand Words

I got a hayfork for the cornfield. May I go by autobus too?

She got a hand lens for the official ornament. The owls may go bye-bye. But she is with the authentic bugle corps city.

Did she rob their bushels of corn? Focus the eye. Do it.

augment augmenter authentic auto autobus aye burl bush cubic

busy bushels but by bye bye-bye cork corn corncob cornfield

cog dogma dognap dorm dormant dory entitle entitlement flame

flam flap flay foal foam fob focus hand lens hang hap height

hayfork hay haughty neurotic owl own owns ox penalty box pen

pen pal pent peptic prism problems prod prodigy proficiency

114a ●
Conditioning Practice
Key each exercise at the right three times.

Alphabetic Practice

Kyle is a scuba diver. How many fathoms can Bridget dive? I plan to jump with Enzo, Tex, and Quinn.

Symbols Practice [* ( )]

k8*k *8k* i8*k l9(l (9l(09(l ;p0))0p;) p0);

114b ● **D**
Evaluation ~ Analysis
Key the timed writing at the right.

Timed Writing

You will require practice keying both the asterisk, *, and the parentheses, (), so that you can key these characters just as quickly as you key the alphabetic characters and numeric characters. Although you might perceive initially that it is unusually difficult to key the asterisk and parentheses at rapid speeds, you must realize that optimum skill growth comes only from repetitive keying practice.

114c Individualized Practice
Key the drill according to the prompts on your screen.

114d WordChamp
Play the game WordChamp.

114e End of Class Procedure . . .
if you are not continuing to the next Session.

Speed Clinic

Symbols

Refer to pages
R-2-R-3 for tips on efficient keying of individual symbols.

*The () is used in computer programs to show the order of how math calculations are to be performed. Check your text now.

k* k* k* ki* ki* i* i* i* k* ki* k* ki* ik* ik* ik* k* k* k*

lo(;p) lo(;p) lo(;p) lo(;p) lo(;p) lo(;p) lo(;p) lo(

(mop) (mop) (mop) (mop) (mop) (mop) (pop) (pop) (pop) (pop)

star * star * star * star * star * *star* *star* *star*

This is the left parenthesis (. This is the right one).

This is a message (look out for typos). (look) (out) (typo)

k* l(;) k* l(;) k* l(;) k* l(;) k* l(;) k* l(;) k* l(

(*) (*) (*) (*) (*) *()* *()* *()* *()* *() (* () () () ***

Session 36—Skillbuilding

36a ●
Conditioning Practice
Key each exercise at the right three times.

Alphabetic Practice
Jack Huffman was able to place every size liquid detergent in six rows.

Digraph Practice (rv mm lu rr cc rc eq nk)
deserve comma luck salute arrange accept arch equal mankind blank

36b ● LA
Evaluation ~ Analysis
Key the timed writing at the right.

Timed Writing
Don't look for an alibi to purchase junk food! It would be an error to think that a good diet is only the result of luck. Health food is a good source of vitamins. You must accept the responsibility to purchase good food from a summer breakfast menu. Your server, at your request, will tell you about the food choices available.

36c Individualized Practice
Key the drill according to the prompts on your screen.

36d WordChamp
Play the game WordChamp.

36e End of Class Procedure . . .
if you are not continuing to the next Session.

Speed Clinic

Did the surveyor survey the curve this summer? For lunch he wants a pink drink. Arrange to accept their parcel request.

rv	curve deserve marvel serve survive surveyor survey interview
mm	comma commerce summer summit command comment grammar summary
lu	lube lug lump lunch lung lurk clue bluff deluxe glued plunge
rr	arrange array arrive arrow berry carry horror hurry occurred
cc	accept accent access accuse succeed account occupy accompany
rc	search starch torch porch parcel mercy force circle circuits
eq	equal equally equip equal equity require request consequence
nk	ankle drink link monkey mink chunk drink pink sink tank bank

Refer to page R-1 for tips on efficient keying of individual letters.

Session 113 — Skillbuilding

113a ●
Conditioning Practice
Key each exercise at the right three times.

Alphabetic Practice

Can Wendy name six of the great books? Shirley found a pair of size seven quality jeans.

Symbols Practice [* ( )]

k8*k *8k* i8*k l9(l (9l(o9(l ;p0))0p;) p0);

113b ● **D**
Evaluation ~ Analysis
Key the timed writing at the right.

Timed Writing

The asterisk, *, may be used in a programming language to denote multiplication. It, the *, is sometimes referred to as the star. The left parenthesis, (, and right parenthesis,), may be used in a programming language to change the order of mathematical calculations. The parentheses, (), are used sometimes to indicate explanatory messages within a program.

113c Individualized Practice
Key the drill according to the prompts on your screen.

113d WordChamp
Play the game WordChamp.

113e End of Class Procedure . . .
if you are not continuing to the next Session.

Speed Clinic

Symbols

The asterisk, (*), is a symbol that may be used to alert us to a footnote.

k* k* k* ki* ki* i* i* i* k* ki* k* ki* ik* ik* ik* k* k* k*

lo(;p) lo(;p) lo(;p) lo(;p) lo(;p) lo(;p) lo(;p) lo(

(mop) (mop) (mop) (mop) (mop) (mop) (pop) (pop) (pop) (pop)

star * star * star * star * star * *star* *star* *star*

This is the left parenthesis (. This is the right one).

This is a message (look out for typos). (look) (out) (typo)

k* l(;) k* l(;) k* l(;) k* l(;) k* l(;) k* l(;) k* l(

(*) (*) (*) (*) (*) *()* *()* *()* *()* *() (* () () () ***

Refer to pages R-2-R-3 for tips on efficient keying of individual symbols.

Session 37—Skillbuilding

37a •
Conditioning Practice
Key each exercise at the right three times.

Alphabetic Practice
Jim was to give each child an exact, equal-sized portion of birthday cake.

Digraph Practice (nu ug go bi ib)
number revenue menu ugly laugh rug goal forgot ago bid cabinet fibers rib

37b • LA
Evaluation ~ Analysis
Key the timed writing at the right.

Timed Writing
Muffins that provide fiber and nuts, fresh fruit, and eggs are only a few things you might have available to begin each morning. Your size will help you gauge the amount of food you need. Never quit! Take a little extra time to make excellent food choices. It is your responsibility to have good food. Good food will help you stay in good health!

37c Individualized Practice
Key the drill according to the prompts on your screen.

37d WordChamp
Play the game WordChamp.

37e End of Class Procedure . . .
if you are not continuing to the next Session.

Speed Clinic

The nurse took a baby rabbit to the nursery. What are their goals for golf? I caught six ugly bugs. Please skip to the bills for the big library debt. He has a habit of eating my peanuts. Call the librarian for my bibliography. They want a gold ribbon, not a free golf game. Does their rabbit bite?

nu nuts nurse number nursery peanut unused tenure bonus unusual

ug ugly bugs caught fought plugs rug rugs plug jug dug drug lug

go go goal gods goes gold golf gone gown jargon agony ago cargo

bi bite birth bill bind bits big debit cubic orbit rabbit habit

ib nibble describe alibi fiber library ribbon edible fibers rib

Refer to page **R-1** for tips on efficient keying of individual letters.

Session 112—Skillbuilding

112a •
Conditioning Practice

Key each exercise at the right three times.

Alphabetic Practice

I bought a PC with a modem, fax, and monitor for their zoo. In seven years Jake will quit.

Symbols Practice (% ^ &)

f5%f %5f% 5%f5 f6^f ^6f^ 6^f6 j7&j &7j& 7&j7

112b • D
Evaluation ~ Analysis

Key the timed writing at the right.

Timed Writing

Judy understood that the ^ symbol was referred to as a circumflex; the & symbol was called the ampersand; and the % symbol denotes a percentage. The ^ is positioned over particular vowels in a word to reveal something about the word's pronunciation; the & is sometimes used in legal names of companies; and the % is commonly found within tabular matter, correspondence, and in forms where space is restricted. Judy's mastery of typographical symbols, her background, and her experience will enable her to advance to higher-level positions with this organization.

112c Individualized Practice

Key the drill according to the prompts on your screen.

112d WordChamp

Play the game WordChamp.

112e End of Class Procedure . . .

if you are not continuing to the next Session.

Speed Clinic

Symbols

Discounts can range from 10% to 35%. Some may offer 15%.

Call the firm of Law & Holm. Learn the use of the ^ today.

f% f% f% fr% fr% r% r% r% f% fr% f% fr% rf% rf% rf% f% f% f%

j^ j^ j^ jy^ jy^ y^ y^ y^ y^ j^ jy^ j^ jy^ yj^ yj^ yj^ j^ j^

j& j& j& ju& ju& u& u& u& j& ju& j& ju& uj& uj uj& j& j& j&

fr% fr% fr% fr% jy^ jy^ jy^ jy^ jy^ ju& ju& ju& ju& ju& ju&

far% fat% far% fat% far% fat% far% fat% far% fat% far% fat%

judy^ judy^ judy^ judy^ judy^ judy^ judy^ judy^ judy^ judy^

guy& guy& guy& guy& guy& guy& guy& guy& guy& guy& guy& guy&

%^& %^& %^& %^& %^& %^& %^& %^& %^& %^& %^& %^& %^& %^& %^& %^&

Refer to pages R-2-R-3 for tips on efficient keying of individual symbols.

Session 38 — Skillbuilding

38a ●
Conditioning Practice

Key each exercise at the right three times.

Alphabetic Practice
Rex W. Beck just gave quite a large sum of money for a charity door prize.

Digraph Practice (ki ub mb ey rk ru pt ht)
kind skill ski ubiquity cube stub symbol climb eye keyboard honey marks work rug truth empty kept eighty right

38b ● LA
Evaluation ~ Analysis

Key the timed writing at the right.

Timed Writing

Davey wanted to purchase a new ruby ring for his wife for their eighth anniversary; however, picking one was very difficult. First, he did not know what size was needed. He also quickly found that most rings were just too expensive. He did not accept the claim by the clerk who told him that the price would soon climb because the market was not very good.

38c Individualized Practice
Key the drill according to the prompts on your screen.

38d WordChamp
Play the game WordChamp.

38e End of Class Procedure . . .
if you are not continuing to the next Session.

Speed Clinic

The member's kid needs clubs. The truth is they cost money.

The captain works at night. Their attorney is Lester Law.

ki	kick kid kills kinds kink kits kind kilo skip cookies asking
ub	clubs cube cubic double doubt lube rubber tub stub club stub
mb	symbol member lambs combat chamber jumbo climb succumb climb
ey	eye eyed eyes eyesight they money turkey key jockey attorney
rk	works worker sparkle parked market fork work lurk spark mark
ru	rug rule run rush rust rut fruit drum true truth virus rerun
pt	captain empty prompts aptly kept adapt tempt prompt kept apt
ht	fights lighter lights mighty rights night might tight taught

Refer to page R-I for tips on efficient keying of individual letters.

111a •
Conditioning Practice
Key each exercise at the right three times.

Alphabetic Practice

Hank and Zack won the most tournaments last year except for Bill. I was quick to judge the victory.

Symbol Practice (\)

;\; \;\ ;\; \;\ ;\; \;\ ;\; \;\ ;\; \;\ ;\; \;\

111b • D
Evaluation ~ Analysis
Key the timed writing at the right.

Timed Writing

Judy Zimpher recently graduated from a journalism program at community college in Miami, Florida. Judy was quickly employed by a publishing company in an entry-level position as a proofreader. Having learned the meaning of the many symbols, such as command \, on the expanded microcomputer keyboard, and her ability to use a variety of applications software made her job with the high-technology publishing company much easier.

111c Individualized Practice
Key the drill according to the prompts on your screen.

111d WordChamp
Play the game WordChamp.

111e End of Class Procedure . . .
if you are not continuing to the next Session.

Speed Clinic

Symbols

The \ symbol is used to display program options on your new computer. Find the \ symbol on your keyboard. Type it too.

;\; ;\; ;\; ;\; ;\; ;\; ;\; ;\; ;\; ;\; ;\; ;\; ;\; ;\; ;\;

;\\; ;\\; ;\\; ;\\; ;\\; ;\\; ;\\; ;\\; ;\\; ;\\; ;\\; ;\\;

pop\ mop\ pop\ mop\ pop\ mop\ pop\ mop\ pop\ mop\ pop\ mop\

soap;\ soap;\ soap;\ soap;\ soul;\ soul;\ soul;\ soul;\

This symbol \ is on your keyboard. Type this symbol \\\\\\.

Type this on your screen cut \ paste \ edit \ print \ save \

The \ symbol is very useful in working your programs. Okay!

Katelyn tried to find the \ symbol on her keyboard as well.

Refer to pages R-2-R-3 for tips on efficient keying of individual symbols.

39a ●

Conditioning Practice

Key each exercise at the right three times.

Alphabetic Practice

Kevin P. Bay just realized the taxi cab fare quoted was above the legal limits.

Digraph Practice (mu pu nv nf tl)

much formula mud put computer input invoice convex conflict confer atlas gentle

---

39b ● LA

Evaluation ~ Analysis

Key the timed writing at the right.

Timed Writing

The maximum amount Davey could pay was five hundred dollars. He flatly refused to pay any more because he had already pulled together all the money he had available for the anniversary gift. He got very involved and was able to find a quite good ruby ring for a fair price. He had the clerk confirm the price of five hundred dollars.

39c Individualized Practice

Key the drill according to the prompts on your screen.

39d WordChamp

Play the game WordChamp.

39e End of Class Procedure . . .

if you are not continuing to the next Session.

Speed Clinic

The public wants the music muted, not at its optimum. Pupils must invest in a computer. The rainfall ruined the canvas.

Use the atlas to make an outline of the puzzle. Invite them to perform an inventory of all public records. The deputy's computer was in the workmen's workshop for needed repairs.

mu	much mud muffle mule music must muted optimum smudge maximum
pu	put push puzzle public puff pull pupil computer deputy input
nv	canvas invite invoice envy invest involve inventory envelope
nf	unfold rainfall unfair infants confine inform influx painful
tl	atlas cattle kettle outline rattle settle quietly apparently

Refer to page **R-1** for tips on efficient keying of individual letters.

Session 110—Assessment

110a
Conditioning Practice

Key the exercise at the right three times.

Alphabetic Practices

You will be amazed and happy with his request. Kevin can exercise five mornings with Jill.

Vi told Quinn and Jim they need more practice with Suzie and Kim before the next golf exam.

What made Bev a success in sports? Was it just hard work or zeal to excel? Finally Virgil quit.

Do you know your city, state, and zip? I live in Newark, NJ. Mr. Max B. High is from Queens, NY.

110b ● Ⓐ
Evaluation ~ Progress

Key the first timed writing at the right.

110c ● Ⓐ
Evaluation ~ Progress

Key the second timed writing at the right.

110d ●
WordChamp

Play the game WordChamp.

110e ●
End of Class Procedure . . .

if you are not continuing to the next Session.

Speed Clinic

Timed Writing

Much research is taking place today to bring to the business world new and better types of communication devices. Just imagine the mix of devices available today. Can you think of any? It is amazing how we have progressed in our quest to establish better contacts with other people. No doubt the future will bring many more unique and wonderful devices for us to use.

Timed Writing

Good communication skills plus good work habits equals advancement for you in not just rank but in pay as well. You should realize that skill in oral communication is necessary in order to do effective work on the job. And effective work on the job could mean a promotion for you. By practicing good oral skills, you can expect to achieve. Remember, practice makes perfect.

Are you planning on attending college after graduation? If the answer is yes then you need to begin planning soon after graduation. Will you attend a college in your state? Or is it a college in another state?

Regardless of your choice we know you will make the right choice. Talk to those who are attending the college of your choice. Visit the campus too. Look at the curriculum.

Does the college have the programs you wish to pursue? If so, write for a catalog and study it so that you will have an idea of what is required. Finally, make sure you know what it will cost to attend. Good luck!

Session 40 — Assessment

40a ●
Conditioning Practice
Key the exercise at the right three times.

Alphabetic Practices

Jack Huffman was able to place every size liquid detergent in six rows.

Jim was to give each child an exact, equal-sized portion of birthday cake.

Rex W. Beck just gave quite a large sum of money for a charity door prize.

Kevin P. Bay just realized the taxi cab fare quoted was above the legal limits.

40b ● (LA)
Evaluation ~ Progress
Key the first timed writing at the right.

40c ● (LA)
Evaluation ~ Progress
Key the second timed writing at the right.

Timed Writing

The world of boating has many aspects to it. You can go sailing or you can use power. You can go cruising or you can go fishing. Whatever your choice of recreational boating, it can be safer and much more enjoyable if it is done with the knowledge of good boating procedures. Quiz yourself on how to use a sextant and a radio. Finally, learn all the boating terms you can before you buy your first boat.

Timed Writing

Golf is a game for all of us to enjoy. In the beginning, it had been played only on courses made by nature. Today we play on beautiful grounds designed and built by professional golfers. Golf can be said to be rewarding, frustrating, and addictive. Yes, it is all of these things; but it is a challenge as well. Also keep in mind that it is a great equalizer. There are very few experts among us. However, we can all have the pleasure of being in the great outdoors when we play golf.

40d ●
WordChamp
Play the game WordChamp.

40e ●
End of Class Procedure . . .
if you are not continuing to the next Session.

Speed Clinic

Balanced-Hand Words

The fog is downtown. Format the six disks. Tow their ruby rug to the downtown official. I got a turn on the autobus.

The heir is a lame duck city official. Rub the cub's eye.

With a yell the visitor and the widow did a turn in the fog.

cot cow cowl cozy cub cubicle dot down downfield downtown to

downright downturn envy eye eye lens entity foe fog for fork

forms formal format fowl heir held hem hen hey he's protozoa

proficient profit proviso row rub ruby rue rug rush rusk rut

109a ●
Conditioning Practice

Key each exercise at the right three times.

Alphabetic Practice

Do you know your city, state, and zip? I live in Newark, NJ. Mr. Max B. High is from Queens, NY.

Symbols Practice (@ # $)

sw2@ @2ws w2@s de3# #3ed e3#d fr4$ $4rf r4$f

109b ● Ⓓ
Evaluation ~ Analysis

Key the timed writing at the right.

Timed Writing

Janet also discovered that eight dozen #2 pencils @ $1.09 were extended to $8.27 instead of $8.72. Finally, 17 reams of 24# paper @ $4.56 a ream were extended to $67.52 instead of $77.52. Janet enjoyed doing this assignment because she did truly like to work with figures, and she appreciated that finding nearly every error is very critical.

109c Individualized Practice

Key the drill according to the prompts on your screen.

109d WordChamp

Play the game WordChamp.

109e End of Class Procedure . . .

if you are not continuing to the next Session.

Speed Clinic

Symbols

Invoice #80 for $441 was lost in the shipment on June 19. I bought a computer with a serial number of @0190634 on July 1.

s@ s@ s@ sw@ sw@ w@ w@ w@ s@ sw@ s@ sw@ ws@ ws@ ws@ s@ s@ s@

f$ f$ f$ fr$ fr$ r$ r$ r$ f$ fr$ f$ fr$ fr$ rf$ rf$ f$ f$ f$

s@f$ s@f$ s@f$ s@f$ s@f$ f$s@ f$s@ f$s@ f$s@ f$s@ @$ @$ @$

sw@ fr$ sw@ fr$ sw@ fr$ sw@ fr$ sw@ fr$ sw@ fr$ sw@ fr$ sw@

d# d# d# de# de# e# e# e# d# de# d# de# ed# ed# ed# ed# d#

ded# ded# ded# ded# ded# de3# de3# de3# de3# ded3# ded# de3#

$100 $200 $300 $400 $500 $600 $700 $800 $900 $123 $456 $789

10 @ 50; 20 @ 65; 100 @ 80; 70 boxes @ 50 cents; 900 @ 300.

Refer to pages R-2-R-3 for tips on efficient keying of individual symbols.

Session 41—Skillbuilding

41a ●
Conditioning Practice
Key each exercise at the right three times.

Alphabetic Practice
Pamela Fay was quick to join others who vetoed the business zone tax package.

Digraph Practice (oi nn ob ms au iz)
oil choice annual inn object globe job himself aims auction beauty bureau size quiz

41b ● LA
Evaluation ~ Analysis
Key the timed writing at the right.

Timed Writing
Annually, many people find themselves in a position in which they weigh just a little too much and think that they must join one of the many organizations that will help them lose the gained weight. Most of these organizations claim that many people gain weight because of their job, their urge to eat food that represents a poor food choice, or the fact that they very often eat more high-calorie food than they realize.

41c Individualized Practice
Key the drill according to the prompts on your screen.

41d WordChamp
Play the game WordChamp.

41e End of Class Procedure . . .
if you are not continuing to the next Session.

Speed Clinic

The ointments can soil the robe. Autumn is a beautiful time to observe the crimson leaves. The winner of the last quiz gets a pizza prize. Did you finalize the autumn trip to our farm or are we going to haul the soil to the city annex?

oi   oil oils ointments void voices toil soil point coil invoices

nn   annex cannot winner penny antenna dinner funny inner flannel

ob   object observe obtain robe probe robot robbed mobile mob job

ms   crimson himself circumstance rooms gems farms elms restrooms

au   autumn autos authors authority beautiful haul caution bureau

iz   citizens pizzas prizes itemized finalized realize pizza quiz

Refer to page **R-1** for tips on efficient keying of individual letters.

Session 108—Skillbuilding

108a ●
Conditioning Practice

Key each exercise at the right three times.

Alphabetic Practice

What made Bev a success in sports? Was it just hard work or zeal to excel? Finally Virgil quit.

Symbols Practice (@ $)

sw2@ @2ws w2@s fr4$ $4rf r4$f sw2@ @2ws w2@s fr4$ $4rf r4$f

108b ● Ⓓ
Evaluation ~ Analysis

Key the timed writing at the right.

Timed Writing

Only Janet Evans was also assigned the critical duty of verifying all of the invoices that were received in the front business office every week. She quickly discovered numerous, serious errors almost every week. Seven printer ribbons @ $4.89 each were extended to $34.32 instead of $34.23.

108c Individualized Practice

Key the drill according to the prompts on your screen.

108d WordChamp

Play the game WordChamp.

108e End of Class Procedure . . .

if you are not continuing to the next Session.

Speed Clinic

Symbols

Refer to pages R-2-R-3 for tips on efficient keying of individual symbols.

The invoice read 21 bottles @ 58 cents each. I bought 2000 @ 10 cents each. I paid $180 for the coat. They cost $168.

s@ s@ s@ sw@ sw@ w@ w@ w@ s@ sw@ s@ sw@ ws@ ws@ ws@ s@ s@ s@

f$ f$ f$ fr$ fr$ r$ r$ r$ f$ fr$ f$ fr$ fr$ rf$ rf$ f$ f$ f$

s@f$ s@f$ s@f$ s@f$ s@f$ f$s@ f$s@ f$s@ f$s@ f$s@ @$ @$ @$

sw@ fr$ sw@ fr$ sw@ fr$ sw@ fr$ sw@ fr$ sw@ fr$ sw@ fr$ sw@

$100 $200 $300 $400 $500 $600 $700 $800 $900 $123 $456 $789

10 @ 50; 20 @ 65; 100 @ 80; 70 boxes @ 50 cents; 900 @ 300.

Session 42—Skillbuilding

42a ●
Conditioning Practice

Key each exercise at the right three times.

Alphabetic Practice
Jim V. Waco quit before realizing his dream to make next year's polo team.

Digraph Practice (rg ud xp og ys oa)
cargo emergency study proud expand biology catalog systems sprays oath boards

42b ● LA
Evaluation ~ Analysis

Key the timed writing at the right.

Timed Writing
No magic pill will cause you to lose weight. You must set a goal weight for yourself and always expect to spend several weeks to realize it. Take the time to exclude any food that is not good for you, to develop a good exercise program, and to develop a good attitude. You will then quickly see the success that no organization can promise!

42c Individualized Practice
Key the drill according to the prompts on your screen.

42d WordChamp
Play the game WordChamp.

42e End of Class Procedure . . .
if you are not continuing to the next Session.

Speed Clinic

It was urgent that we send the large cargo on the barge. We expect the taxpayer to pay the expense. Marge is our dog.

Study the budget to stop fraud. Can I watch the geyser from their sailboat? Rachel jogs with our dog Marge. So do I.

rg	urgent surge organ forge cargo barge urge large charge organ
ud	study buds audio budget puddle studying loud fraud proud mud
xp	expand expect expire explain taxpayer expert explore expense
og	jogs logic slogan apology logs logical loges hog nog jog dog
ys	geyser system analysis stays trays toys buys plays says ways
oa	oak oaks oat oath oats throat soap road toast roads sailboat

Refer to page R-1 for tips on efficient keying of individual letters.

107a
Conditioning Practice
Key each exercise at the right three times.

Alphabetic Practice
Vi told Quinn and Jim they need more practice with Suzie and Kim before the next golf exam.

Numbers Practice (7 8 9)
ju7 ki8 lo9 7uj 8ik 9ol u7j i8k o9l uj7 ik8 ol9

107b ● D
Evaluation ~ Analysis
Key the timed writing at the right.

Timed Writing
Gerald realized he could change the type of printer to a laser printer for an additional $279.33. The system he finally decided to purchase included the following software applications: database, word processing, and spreadsheet. Gerald was really quite excited about the new microcomputer system he just purchased. He learned most of the software applications in only five days.

107c Individualized Practice
Key the drill according to the prompts on your screen.

107d WordChamp
Play the game WordChamp.

107e End of Class Procedure . . .
if you are not continuing to the next Session.

Speed Clinic

Numbers

The airport gate number is B9. Flight 798 will arrive at 10 p.m. I live at 800 Augusta Rd. I lived at 1260 Clubview.

j7 j7 j7 ju7 ju7 u7 u7 u7 j7 ju7 j7 ju7 uj7 uj7 uj7 j7 j7 j7

k8 k8 k8 ki8 ki8 i8 i8 i8 k8 ki8 k8 ki8 ik8 ik8 ik8 k8 k8 k8

l9 l9 l9 lo9 lo9 o9 o9 o9 l9 lo9 l9 lo9 ol9 ol9 ol9 l9 l9 l9

j7 k8 l9 j7 k8 l9 j7 k8 l9 j7 k8 l9 j7 k8 l9 j7 k8 l9 j7 k8

789 789 789 789 789 789 789 789 789 789 789 789 789 789 789

897 897 897 897 897 897 897 897 897 897 897 897 897 897 897

j7k8l9 j7k8l9 j7k8l9 j7k8l9 j7k8l9 j7k8l9 j7k8l9 j7k8l9 789

mom9 mil8 jug7 mom9 mil8 jug7 mom9 mil8 jug7 mom9 mil8 jug7

Refer to pages R-3-R-4 for tips on efficient keying of individual numbers.

Session 43 — Skillbuilding

43a ●
Conditioning Practice
Key each exercise at the right three times.

Alphabetic Practice
Doug W. Carvey just asked about the size of the quite large tax payment.

Digraph Practice (lt dr ok wn vo nl dv)
faculty consult drove hundred okay broke yearbook owner known void involve unless advance

---

43b ● **LA**
Evaluation ~ Analysis
Key the timed writing at the right.

Timed Writing
For a long time now, many doctors have advised their patients to stop smoking. In addition, many towns have voted to only permit it in a few very restricted areas. Each person must realize that he or she must address this problem as it relates to his or her own good health.

43c Individualized Practice
Key the drill according to the prompts on your screen.

43d WordChamp
Play the game WordChamp.

43e End of Class Procedure . . .
if you are not continuing to the next Session.

Speed Clinic

Did you get advice on a book for your children? I drove our car to the town inlet. As an adult you can vote. The owner was vocal in his advice to the town's children. It is okay.

lt belts health rebuilt guilty adult quilt salt vault tilt volt

dr dry drum drove driver dream hydro children bedroom withdrawn

ok okay broke broken broker joke smoke book shook brook outlook

wn gowns owned owner owns towns own gown brown town down thrown

vo void volts vote voice vocal avoid divorce favor havoc revoke

nl enlist inlets unless evenly only unlike mainly inlet humanly

dv adviser advisory advance advice advise advocate disadvantage

Refer to page R-1 for tips on efficient keying of individual letters.

106a ●
Conditioning Practice
Key each exercise at the right three times.

Alphabetic Practice

You will be amazed and happy with his request. Kevin can exercise five mornings with Jill.

Numbers Practice (7 8 9)

ju7 ki8 lo9 7uj 8ik 9ol u7j i8k o9l uj7 ik8 ol9

106b ● Ⓓ
Evaluation ~ Analysis
Key the timed writing at the right.

Timed Writing

Gerald Wadsworth wanted to purchase an electronic typewriter to take with him to the university. Gerald's mother thought a more practical solution would be to purchase a microcomputer system with a word processing software package. Gerald could purchase a complete microcomputer system for $1398.79.

106c Individualized Practice
Key the drill according to the prompts on your screen.

106d WordChamp
Play the game WordChamp.

106e End of Class Procedure . . .
if you are not continuing to the next Session.

Speed Clinic

Numbers

Refer to pages **R-3-R-4** for tips on efficient keying of individual numbers.

Stacey found that 85 to 90 contracts are missing from their files. My new extension is 679. My old extension was 158.

j7 j7 j7 ju7 ju7 u7 u7 u7 j7 ju7 j7 ju7 uj7 uj7 uj7 j7 j7 j7

k8 k8 k8 ki8 ki8 i8 i8 i8 k8 ki8 k8 ki8 ik8 ik8 ik8 k8 k8 k8

l9 l9 l9 lo9 lo9 o9 o9 o9 l9 lo9 l9 lo9 ol9 ol9 ol9 l9 l9 l9

j7 k8 l9 j7 k8 l9 j7 k8 l9 j7 k8 l9 j7 k8 l9 j7 k8 l9 j7 k8

789 789 789 789 789 789 789 789 789 789 789 789 789 789 789

897 897 897 897 897 897 897 897 897 897 897 897 897 897 897

j7k8l9 j7k8l9 j7k8l9 j7k8l9 j7k8l9 j7k8l9 j7k8l9 j7k8l9 789

mom9 mil8 jug7 mom9 mil8 jug7 mom9 mil8 jug7 mom9 mil8 jug7

44a ●
Conditioning Practice
Key each exercise at the right three times.

Alphabetic Practice
Jacob F. Kelly was very excited to go participate in the unique math quiz.

Digraph Practice (af kn tm br dd ks tw)
after safety deaf knew unknown utmost bring added odd workshop asks twice

44b ● LA
Evaluation ~ Analysis
Key the timed writing at the right.

Timed Writing
Keep in mind that many smoker workshops are staffed by excellent people who know how to help you to stop smoking. Break this bad habit. There is no middle-of-the-road position. You either smoke, or you don't. Quit now; it is of the utmost importance! It will just be twice as difficult in the future.

44c Individualized Practice
Key the drill according to the prompts on your screen.

44d WordChamp
Play the game WordChamp.

44e End of Class Procedure . . .
if you are not continuing to the next Session.

Speed Clinic

After my accident I needed a knee brace. My broker said she knew of the investment. Folks at the bookstore added twenty new workshops. My treatment was after the twentieth of May.

af	affair affect affix afford after safe traffic leaf loaf deaf
kn	knack knee knew knife knight knit knot know unknown weakness
tm	utmost treatment postmark investment atmosphere appointments
br	broom broker brief breath brace debris embrace hombre embryo
dd	sudden peddle adds middle midday hidden bladder odds odd add
ks	workshop bookstore asks folks inks looks speaks thanks decks
tw	twelve twenties twentieth twenty twice two between outwardly

Refer to page R-1 for tips on efficient keying of individual letters.

105a ●

Conditioning Practice

Key the exercise at the right three times.

Alphabetic Practices

Some of these words have double letters: skiing, pizza, puppy, affix, cuff, jug, mom, quo.

A good quality of life is important to everyone of us. Zeke was lax with his bike. Jack was too.

Work hard and expect to achieve. Seize the moment. Bill and Jill are first in your goal quest.

People who exercise feel good about themselves. Yolanda and Jack have the zeal to qualify.

105b ● Ⓐ

Evaluation ~ Progress

Key the first timed writing at the right.

105c ● Ⓐ

Evaluation ~ Progress

Key the second timed writing at the right.

105d ●

WordChamp

Play the game WordChamp.

105e ●

End of Class Procedure . . .

if you are not continuing to the next Session.

Speed Clinic

Timed Writing

Throughout our history writing has taken many forms, from the primitive marks on cave walls to the most sophisticated word processing programs of today. But always the goal has been communication. In just the past few years, there has been an amazing explosion in the kinds of computer equipment available to help us in our day-to-day lives. Can you name some of these?

Timed Writing

To know about boats you need to understand the special words and phrases that make up the field of boating. Do you know the meaning of these words: jib, quay, sextant, capsize? Learning and using proper nautical terms will identify you as one who is truly interested in boating. Above all, form the habit of thinking in nautical terms as much as possible. Soon the correct words will come naturally.

You should be getting ready for a new school year. Today is a good time to begin. Make sure you have the appropriate or necessary clothes for classes.

Get your writing materials. And be sure you know what your schedule will be. Yes, it is important to be prepared. Also check with your friends. We know that many of them may need help also.

Will you take a bus or do you plan on driving your own car? Insurance is an important decision.

Keep in mind that your success in class is dependent on how hard you plan to work. Study hard! Go to every class, and you will be amazed on how time passes.

Session 45—Assessment

45a •

Conditioning Practice

Key the exercise at the right three times.

Alphabetic Practices

Pamela Fay was quick to join others who vetoed the business zone tax package.

Jim V. Waco quit before realizing his dream to make next year's polo team.

Doug W. Carvey just asked about the size of the quite large tax payment.

Jacob F. Kelly was very excited to go participate in the unique math quiz.

45b • **A**

Evaluation ~ Progress

Key the first timed writing at the right.

45c • **A**

Evaluation ~ Progress

Key the second timed writing at the right.

45d •

WordChamp

Play the game WordChamp.

45e •

End of Class Procedure . . .

if you are not continuing to the next Session.

Timed Writing

If you feel good about yourself, chances are you are happier, more positive, and more likely to achieve your ambitions and objectives in life. A good quality of life is important to every one of us. Work hard and expect to achieve. Remember to seize the moment.

Timed Writing

While each of us is a unique person, we all recognize that exercise is an important routine in our daily life. People who exercise regularly feel good about themselves. They have better memories and better reaction times than those who do not exercise. Just plan to keep fit.

Speed Clinic

Balanced-Hand Words

The ducks may smell the foxy fox. The snake is due. She cut the small turkey. Smell the fuel by their town lake. May I name the small fox Fuchsia? I kept them by the busy island.

cubit cud cue curl cusp cuss cut cuticle cycle dual dub duck

duck due duel dug dusk duty dye fox foxy fuchsia fuel prowls

fur furl furor fury prow proxy prudish psyche slant slap she

slay sleigh sleight sleuth small smell snake snap sleight of

hand so soak soap sob social socks tow to wit towns toxic to

tub tuck tug turkey turns turndown tusks tyro world worm wow

sod sorority sorrow sorry sow spa span spangle spell suspend

Session 104 — Skillbuilding

104a ●
Conditioning Practice
Key each exercise at the right three times.

Alphabetic Practice
People who exercise feel good about themselves. Yolanda and Jack have the zeal to qualify.

Numbers Practice (4 5 6)
fr4 gt5 hy6 4rf 5tg 6yh r4f t5g y6h rf4 tg5 hy6

104b ● Ⓓ
Evaluation ~ Analysis
Key the timed writing at the right.

Timed Writing
Fortunately for Caroline, one college in San Francisco, California, quoted a price that was considerably less than the others. She could attend that university in San Francisco for about $456 less than any other school in the San Francisco, California, area. Caroline realized she could just about afford that university if she saved most of the money she would earn working as a secretary during the summer.

104c Individualized Practice
Key the drill according to the prompts on your screen.

104d WordChamp
Play the game WordChamp.

104e End of Class Procedure . . .
if you are not continuing to the next Session.

Speed Clinic

Numbers

The ticket number was 130456. What city has the ZIP Code of 43210? The temperature at 5 p.m. was 54 degrees back home.

f4 f4 f4 fr4 fr4 r4 r4 r4 f4 fr4 f4 fr4 rf4 rf4 rf4 f4 f4 f4

f5 f5 f5 ft5 ft5 t5 t5 t5 f5 ft5 f5 ft5 ft5 tf5 tf5 f5 f5 f5

h6 h6 h6 hy6 hy6 y6 y6 y6 h6 hy6 h6 hy6 hy6 yh6 yh6 h6 h6 h6

f4 f5 h6 f4 f5 h6 f4 f5 h6 f4 f5 h6 f4 f5 h6 f4 f5 h6 f4 f5

456 456 456 456 456 456 456 456 456 456 456 456 456 456 456 456

654 654 654 654 654 654 654 654 654 654 654 654 654 654 654 654

f45h6 f45h6 f45h6 h6f45 h6f45 h6f45 f45h6 f45h6 f45h6 456

hot4 hot4 hot4 par5 par5 par5 hay6 hay6 hay6 hot4 par5 hay6

Refer to pages R-3-R-4 for tips on efficient keying of individual numbers.

Session 46—Skillbuilding

46a ●
Conditioning Practice
Key each exercise at the right three times.

Alphabetic Practice
Wanda Black kept every exam and major quiz from geography class this year.

Digraph Practice (gn hr ze xt ju gu py gs lf)
signal assign three zero sized gaze extra next jug adjust gum figure pyramid copying happy amongst flags fulfill golf

---

46b ● **LA**
Evaluation ~ Analysis
Key the timed writing at the right.

Timed Writing

The sign placed on the wall alongside the public photocopy machine in the new mall said: Buy three dozen copies at the cost of three dollars and get an extra dozen for just half the regular price. The sign also warned anyone using the copy machine to be very careful not to violate any federal copyright law.

46c Individualized Practice
Key the drill according to the prompts on your screen.

46d WordChamp
Play the game WordChamp.

46e End of Class Procedure . . .
if you are not continuing to the next Session.

Speed Clinic

Type these: sign, three, zero, text, jugs, gum, copy, gulf.

gn signed signs signal sign design redesign assign foreign sign

hr thrill threads shrimp throw shreds chrome three threw thrift

ze zest zero dozen prizes prize size glaze maze amaze gaze maze

xt fixture textbooks texts sixteen texture mixture text context

ju jug jump junior just juice juror junk adjust adjuncts injury

gu guys gum guide guess gun gulp guard gums gulf argue argument

py pyramid pyres shipyard copying spyglasses sloppy skimpy copy

gs youngster amongst drugstore wings tags sings rings rigs logs

lf golfing unselfish halfway billfold welfare calf gulf twelfth

Refer to page **R-1** for tips on efficient keying of individual letters.

Session 103 — Skillbuilding

103a ●
Conditioning Practice
Key each exercise at the right three times.

Alphabetic Practice
Work hard and expect to achieve. Seize the moment. Bill and Jill are first in your goal quest.

Numbers Practice (4 5 6)
fr4 gt5 hy6 4rf 5tg 6yh r4f t5g y6h rf4 tg5 hy6

103b ● **D**
Evaluation ~ Analysis
Key the timed writing at the right.

Timed Writing
Caroline D'Noffrio sent a letter to the university to inquire about tuition for one semester. She received a response stating that the tuition was currently $1456, but would be increased to $1654 next semester. Caroline felt the current tuition of $1456 was exorbitant and made numerous inquiries at other schools. Every college or university responded to her inquiry. The tuition seemed about equivalent.

103c Individualized Practice
Key the drill according to the prompts on your screen.

103d WordChamp
Play the game WordChamp.

103e End of Class Procedure . . .
if you are not continuing to the next Session.

Speed Clinic

Numbers

On June 16, 55 new state employees will be added. I need 44 instead of 66. When I arrived in Florida it was 65 degrees.

f4 f4 f4 fr4 fr4 r4 r4 r4 f4 fr4 f4 fr4 rf4 rf4 rf4 f4 f4 f4

f5 f5 f5 ft5 ft5 t5 t5 t5 f5 ft5 f5 ft5 ft5 tf5 tf5 f5 f5 f5

h6 h6 h6 hy6 hy6 y6 y6 y6 h6 hy6 h6 hy6 hy6 yh6 yh6 h6 h6 h6

f4 f5 h6 f4 f5 h6 f4 f5 h6 f4 f5 h6 f4 f5 h6 f4 f5 h6 f4 f5

456 456 456 456 456 456 456 456 456 456 456 456 456 456 456

654 654 654 654 654 654 654 654 654 654 654 654 654 654 654

f45h6 f45h6 f45h6 h6f45 h6f45 h6f45 f45h6 f45h6 f45h6 456

hot4 hot4 hot4 par5 par5 par5 hay6 hay6 hay6 hot4 par5 hay6

Refer to pages R-3-R-4 for tips on efficient keying of individual numbers.

Session 47 — Skillbuilding

47a ●
Conditioning Practice
Key each exercise at the right three times.

Alphabetic Practice
Alex Wu was not lazy; he quickly made four big pizzas in just five minutes.

Digraph Practice (ft oy cy ph wr)
after craft employed joy cycle policyholder agency phone alpha paragraph wrap showroom

---

47b ● (LA)
Evaluation ~ Analysis
Key the timed writing at the right.

Timed Writing
Ruth needed to make a number of copies of a typewritten draft of a policy statement, but the copy machine in her office was not working at this time. Ruth figured she could make all of the copies she needed on the mall machine in about ten minutes. She quickly phoned her employer to get approval.

47c Individualized Practice
Key the drill according to the prompts on your screen.

47d WordChamp
Play the game WordChamp.

47e End of Class Procedure . . .
if you are not continuing to the next Session.

Speed Clinic

On the fifth afternoon the loyal cowboy wrote the playboy an urgent letter. The cyclone wrecked the aircraft. Her photo is by the phone. Call the agency to get the data from Jeff.

What has this writer written? If she is fifty give her the new furnishings she wanted. Is it in the last subparagraph?

ft   after afternoon crafts fifth fiftieth fifty shaft gift drift

oy   boys toys royal loyal alloy enjoy cowboy playboy toy joy boy

cy   cycle cycles cyclones cylinder pharmacy agency fancy urgency

ph   phrase photo phone phrase physics sphere upheld subparagraph

wr   wraps wreck write wrapper writer written wrong wrist unwrap

Refer to page **R-1** for tips on efficient keying of individual letters.

Session 102—Skillbuilding

102a ●
Conditioning Practice

Key each exercise at the right three times.

Alphabetic Practice

A good quality of life is important to every one of us. Zeke was lax with his bike. Jack was too.

Numbers Practice (0 1 2 3)

;p0 aq1 sw2 de3 0p; 1qa 2ws 3ed p0; q1a w2s e3d p;0 qa1 ws2 ed3

102b ● Ⓓ
Evaluation ~ Analysis

Key the timed writing at the right.

Timed Writing

The actual amount of money that Anthony finally paid for his new mower was exactly $23.10 less than the price of the same, exact lawn mower quoted at a competitor's store in Monroeville, Pennsylvania. Paying only $310.23 seemed justification for all of the excessive time Anthony took doing comparison shopping throughout the county.

102c Individualized Practice

Key the drill according to the prompts on your screen.

102d WordChamp

Play the game WordChamp.

102e End of Class Procedure . . .

if you are not continuing to the next Session.

Speed Clinic

Numbers

Refer to pages **R-3-R-4** for tips on efficient keying of individual numbers.

100 plus 11 equals 111. 100 times 10 equals 1000. The area code for my new telephone is 233. Call Ed at 1 p.m. today.

;0 ;0 ;0 ;p0 ;p0 p0 p0 p0 ;0 ;p0 ;0 ;p0 ;p0 ;p0 ;p0 ;0 ;0 ;0

a1 a1 a1 aq1 aq1 q1 q1 q1 a1 aq1 a1 aq1 qa1 qa1 qa1 a1 a1 a1

s2 s2 s2 sw2 sw2 w2 w2 w2 s2 sw2 s2 sw2 ws2 ws2 ws2 s2 s2 s2

d3 d3 d3 de3 de3 e3 e3 e3 d3 de3 d3 de3 de3 de3 ed3 d3 d3 d3

;0 a1 s2 d3 ;0 a1 s2 d3 a123 a123 a123 ;0123 ;0123 ;0123 123

0123 0123 0123 0123 0123 0123 0123 0123 0123 0123 0123 0123

11 22 33 00 11 22 33 00 11 22 33 00 11 22 33 00 11 22 33 00

saw2 dad3 dad0 as2 saw2 dad3 pap0 as2 saw2 dad3 pap0 as2 123

48a •
Conditioning Practice
Key each exercise at the right three times.

Alphabetic Practice
Cliff Mark Volpe just did not find the right size box required by law.

Digraph Practice (rl my jo pm ik rp eo)
girls pearl myself army job enjoy development alike surplus sharp theory stereo

48b • LA
Evaluation ~ Analysis
Key the timed writing at the right.

Timed Writing
Quick air strikes were used early Wednesday morning to stop a major shipment of arms to the enemy. Many people feel that no military action should have been taken to stop the arms delivery. The four-star general in charge said that there was a clear purpose for this action, but he would not give the exact nature of the mission.

48c Individualized Practice
Key the drill according to the prompts on your screen.

48d WordChamp
Play the game WordChamp.

48e End of Class Procedure . . .
if you are not continuing to the next Session.

Speed Clinic

The girls from the academy have good hourly jobs. Unlike my shipmates, I like to hike in the winter wonderland. Many of my friends came to the surprise luncheon at the city center.

rl girls yearly dearly early hourly world wonderland pearl girl

my myself mysteries mystery army academy dummy economy roomy

jo job jobs join joke joy jog jot journal journalist major jobs

pm shipmate shipments shipment equipment development equipment

ik alike like likes hikes spikes liking strikes pike likelihood

rp overpaid corps surprise orphans purpose carpet surplus sharp

eo neon people peony reorder theory pigeon luncheon stereo oleo

Refer to page R-I for tips on efficient keying of individual letters.

Session 101 — Skillbuilding

101a ●
Conditioning Practice
Key each exercise at the right three times.

Alphabetic Practice

Some of these words have double letters: skiing, pizza, puppy, affix, cuff, jug, mom, quo.

Numbers Practice (0 1 2 3)

;p0 aq1 sw2 de3 0p; 1qa 2ws 3ed p0; q1a w2s e3d p;0 qa1 ws2 ed3

101b ● Ⓓ
Evaluation ~ Analysis
Key the timed writing at the right.

Timed Writing

Anthony Bennington of Pittsburgh, Pennsylvania, purchased a brand-new riding lawn mower for only $310.23. He was very delighted that he received a discount equivalent to about 20 percent because the mowing season was just about over. After he inquired about a discount for also paying cash, Anthony realized he did receive an additional 2 percent off the riding mower's retail price.

101c Individualized Practice
Key the drill according to the prompts on your screen.

101d WordChamp
Play the game WordChamp.

101e End of Class Procedure . . .
if you are not continuing to the next Session.

Speed Clinic

Numbers

My tee time is either 1 p.m. or 2 p.m. I like 3 p.m. Susan and I play from tee number 1 or tee number 10. Tee 1 is ok.

;0 ;0 ;0 ;p0 ;p0 p0 p0 p0 ;0 ;p0 ;0 ;p0 ;p0 ;p0 ;p0 ;0 ;0 ;0

a1 a1 a1 aq1 aq1 q1 q1 q1 a1 aq1 a1 aq1 qa1 qa1 qa1 a1 a1 a1

s2 s2 s2 sw2 sw2 w2 w2 w2 s2 sw2 s2 sw2 ws2 ws2 ws2 s2 s2 s2

d3 d3 d3 de3 de3 e3 e3 e3 d3 de3 d3 de3 de3 de3 ed3 d3 d3 d3

;0 a1 s2 d3 ;0 a1 s2 d3 a123 a123 a123 ;0123 ;0123 ;0123 123

0123 0123 0123 0123 0123 0123 0123 0123 0123 0123 0123 0123

11 22 33 00 11 22 33 00 11 22 33 00 11 22 33 00 11 22 33 00

saw2 dad3 dad0 as2 saw2 dad3 pap0 as2 saw2 dad3 pap0 as2 123

Refer to pages R-3-R-4 for tips on efficient keying of individual numbers.

Session 49—Skillbuilding

49a ●
Conditioning Practice
Key each exercise at the right three times.

Alphabetic Practice
Cathy D. Vaper just began by taking an equal-sized mixture of water and flour.

Digraph Practice (lp sk aw dl ym)
alpha help sky asked task await lawn draw friendly anymore gym

49b ● **LA**
Evaluation ~ Analysis
Key the timed writing at the right.

Timed Writing

Senator Zelkin stated, "I saw no need for such action that put our forces at risk! We should not have taken this step at the present time!" Very few members of the Congress supported this symbolic action. Others said that we should not stand idle. The senators said we must look out for ourselves, and we must help our allies.

49c Individualized Practice
Key the drill according to the prompts on your screen.

49d WordChamp
Play the game WordChamp.

49e End of Class Procedure . . .
if you are not continuing to the next Session.

Speed Clinic

The alpine sky made the trip risky. We have to await my law professor before we handle the awkward problem. I found the needle in the middle of the puddle with a paddle. Help her with the wallpaper. I need candles for the symphony. Smoke was seen in the gym. It might have been vandalism. I know.

Refer to page R-1 for tips on efficient keying of individual letters.

lp   alpine dolphin helper sulphur wallpaper alpha pulp help gulp

sk   sky skull skip skin skill ski risks risky cask risk desk ask

aw   await awake award away awful awkward squaw draw saw flaw law

dl   puddle needle idle bundle middle handle sadly paddle candles

ym   hymn payment anymore symbol symphony symbols gym acronym gym

100a ●
Conditioning Practice
Key the exercise at the right three times.

Alphabetic Practices

Jacqueline and Zeb take daily walks. Running is one exciting form of physical activity.

We live in Miami and travel to the Virgin Islands. Becky Z. Fix prefers a quiet jet.

What do these golf words mean: hazard, bogey, chip, divot, xout? Jake quit.

Stacey's wedding invitation was for Saturday at one o'clock. BJ Zorn, Max, and Phil left quietly.

100b ● A
Evaluation ~ Progress
Key the first timed writing at the right.

100c ● A
Evaluation ~ Progress
Key the second timed writing at the right.

100d ●
WordChamp
Play the game WordChamp.

100e ●
End of Class Procedure . . .
if you are not continuing to the next Session.

Timed Writing

Keep it simple. You have heard this said many times. It also applies to writing a letter. You can keep a letter simple by grouping ideas into paragraphs. The paragraphs help organize sentences and also help the reader to receive the desired data. You can quickly identify these letters. You can exercise your writing skills by just writing a letter a day.

Timed Writing

From its very beginning, accounting has required skill and patience. At one time, only those with beautiful penmanship were given the job to keep and record records. Now with the use of computers, the field of accounting has modernized. With the use of a computer we can become experts in keeping and preparing our reports. The computer has made the job much easier for us.

Speed Clinic

One-Hand Words by Letter of Alphabet

The nun is the only one to want a puppy. My pup is white.

In this era fat foods are not a fad. Rest and read before I call for the car.

a bag cab dad eat fad gas him in joy kin lip mom no oh pup

rag sad tab up vat we you zag

ace act bag bar car cat date daze egg era fad fat get gag

hop hook inn ink junk jink kin kilo lion look milk mink noun

nun on only pup puppy rest read see sea tea tee up upon vase

vat was we yip yolk zebra zebras

50a ●
Conditioning Practice
Key the exercise at the right three times.

Alphabetic Practices

Wanda Black kept every exam and major quiz from geography class this year.

Alex Wu was not lazy; he quickly made four big pizzas in just five minutes.

Cliff Mark Volpe just did not find the right size box required by law.

Cathy D. Vaper just began by taking an equal-sized mixture of water and flour.

50b ● Ⓐ
Evaluation ~ Progress
Key the first timed writing at the right.

50c ● Ⓐ
Evaluation ~ Progress
Key the second timed writing at the right.

50d ●
WordChamp
Play the game WordChamp.

50e ●
End of Class Procedure . . .
if you are not continuing to the next Session.

Speed Clinic

Left Hand Words/ Right Hand Words

Timed Writing

For real success in the office, one must possess some degree of confidence in his or her own ability. Employers expect to find this trait in both their new and old employees. As one moves up the company ladder, confidence becomes increasingly important. Do you know what the word confidence means? If not, be quick to inquire. Just remember the prize in store for you if you apply the word.

Timed Writing

The potential ability of a human being is without limit. The average person uses only a small portion of his or her potential ability. In reading the life stories of successful men and women, you will find that, for the most part, their success resulted from ambition and hard work. It did not result from natural ability as one would expect. Examine the lives of a dozen qualified men and women. Is this statement true? Can it be justified?

My ace racer was eager. In my garage I bet my race crews.

I'll be eager to dare the race crew to race in the best car.

My car needs gas. Dad is dressed in his kimono. Mom is the reader in my family. Face east on my hill. I'll face east.

ace hill acre him acres hip bad ill bag imply bags in barge

ink cab inn cabs ion cad join cafe jolly cage joy dab kimono

dad junk dare kill dart kiln darted kilo eager kin ear kinky

ears kink east knoll eat kook eats kooky face lily fact limp

faced link faces lion gab lip gadget loin gag look loom gage

garage loop garb lump gas lumpy race milk raced milky reader

99a ●
Conditioning Practice
Key each exercise at the right three times.

Alphabetic Practice
Stacey's wedding invitation was for Saturday at one o'clock. BJ Zorn, Max, and Phil left quietly.

Digraph Practice (sv xf xo xq)
transversely oxfords inexorably exquisitely transversely oxfords inexorably exquisitely

99b ● **HA**
Evaluation ~ Analysis
Key the timed writing at the right.

Timed Writing
Vincent placed each carton transversely. He was inexorably committed to doing a very good job. His supervisor said that his ability to do a quality job was exquisite. He, too, was rewarded for his outstanding productivity. He would buy new oxfords with his money.

99c Individualized Practice
Key the drill according to the prompts on your screen.

99d WordChamp
Play the game WordChamp.

99e End of Class Procedure . . .
if you are not continuing to the next Session.

Speed Clinic

The word transversely is an adverb. It means crosswise.

They bought a new pair of oxfords. I like oxford shirts.

Is the meaning of inexorable to be inflexible? Check on it.

It was an exquisitely designed piece of modern furniture.

Can you spell the words transversely and inexorably?

How about using the words oxfords and exquisitely together?

Refer to page R-1 for tips on efficient keying of individual letters.

sv transversely transversely transversely transversely transversely

xf oxfords oxfords oxfords oxfords oxfords oxfords oxfords

xo inexorably inexorably inexorably inexorably inexorably

xq exquisitely exquisitely exquisitely exquisitely exquisitely

Session 51—Skillbuilding

51a ●
Conditioning Practice
Key each exercise at the right three times.

Alphabetic Practice
Jacob F. Lomax was very happy to know he got a good score on the quiz.

Digraph Practice (rw xc ek dy ws ax sy)
airways exceed inexcusable eking weekend seek dynamic midyear study lawsuit jaws axle waxing relax symbol psychology easy

51b ● A
Evaluation ~ Analysis
Key the timed writing at the right.

Timed Writing
A skilled handyman knows he must complete quality work no matter how busy he might become. He must excel in his occupation if he contemplates looking forward to a successful, prosperous future. Because a handyman must put forth maximum effort every week, he must also learn to just relax when he is not working.

51c Individualized Practice
Key the drill according to the prompts on your screen.

51d WordChamp
Play the game WordChamp.

51e End of Class Procedure . . .
if you are not continuing to the next Session.

Speed Clinic

The taxpayer had no excuse. Rekey the newspaper symbols. I excused the taxi driver. By midyear I finished the fairway.

The lawsuit was in the newsletter. There are no exceptions.

rw   paperwork waterways airway fairway stairway waterway forward

xc   excuse excess excel excise exceed excused excerpt exceptions

ek   eking seeker rekey weeks weekend pekoe seeks seek week creek

dy   dye dyed dynamic dynamics midyear anybody's body needy study

ws   newspaper newsstand lawsuit newsletter saws crews rows allows

ax   axle axles taxi taxpayer taxicab taxes flax relax ax lax wax

sy   symbol system sympathy symbols syrup busy easy glossy woodsy

Refer to page R-1 for tips on efficient keying of individual letters.

98a ●
Conditioning Practice
Key each exercise at the right three times.

Alphabetic Practice
What do these golf words mean: hazard, bogey, chip, divot, xout? Jake quit.

Digraph Practice (mv oq rj xs zy)
circumvent colloquy overjoyed flaxseed breezy circumvent colloquy overjoyed flaxseed breezy

98b ● **HA**
Evaluation ~ Analysis
Key the timed writing at the right.

Timed Writing
Ronald worked every day picking flaxseed. Flaxseed is often used to make linseed oil. He was not a lazy person, and he was overjoyed when he was told that he earned a bonus for his outstanding daily productivity. He never tried to circumvent the established procedures. During his daily morning break, he read a soliloquy.

98c Individualized Practice
Key the drill according to the prompts on your screen.

98d WordChamp
Play the game WordChamp.

98e End of Class Procedure . . .
if you are not continuing to the next Session.

Speed Clinic

It was a lazy, breezy day on the lake. She was overjoyed.

Flaxseed is the source of linseed oil. It is very useful.

Flaxseed is the seed of flax. It has several useful uses.

Look up the word colloquy in our dictionary. Check its use.

We had to circumvent the bridge due to the massive flooding.

mv   circumvent circumvent circumvent circumvent circumvent

oq   colloquy colloquy colloquy colloquy colloquy colloquy

rj   overjoyed overjoyed overjoyed overjoyed overjoyed overjoyed

xs   flaxseed flaxseed flaxseed flaxseed flaxseed flaxseed

zy   breezy lazy breezy lazy breezy lazy breezy lazy breezy lazy

Refer to page R-1 for tips on efficient keying of individual letters.

Session 52—Skillbuilding

52a ●
Conditioning Practice
Key each exercise at the right three times.

Alphabetic Practice
Paula F. Gabor liked very much to relax while enjoying quality jazz music.

Digraph Practice (sm bs ps gl je gg)
smart cosmetics realism absent tabs psychologist elapse stamps glad angle jeans subject luggage egg

---

52b ● Ⓐ
Evaluation ~ Analysis
Key the timed writing at the right.

Timed Writing
Zeb presently works as a handyman for a small manufacturing company; he has only been absent a single day during the last several years! He is a small, yet rugged man. He was not upset when Charles, the supervisor at his company, assigned him to complete a special project. Zeb thought the project would take several days to complete.

52c Individualized Practice
Key the drill according to the prompts on your screen.

52d WordChamp
Play the game WordChamp.

52e End of Class Procedure . . .
if you are not continuing to the next Session.

Speed Clinic

The small luggage was in the baggage area. I object to his psychology class. Do jewels and jeans go together? Can you transmit the job data around the globe? I was glad the jobs were in the suburbs. Do you want one egg or two eggs?

sm   small smaller smart smarter smear transmit realism communism

bs   absent absolute absorb observe bulbs jobs stubs suburbs tabs

ps   psychology lapsed snapshot caps pops ups wraps bumps wallops

gl   glad glass glaze globe glove glassware igloo wiggle triangle

je   jeans jet jewels jewelers jerseys jeans inject object reject

gg   wiggle luggage trigger rugged eggs buggy baggage plugged egg

Refer to page R-1 for tips on efficient keying of individual letters.

Session 97—Skillbuilding

97a ●
Conditioning Practice

Key each exercise at the right three times.

Alphabetic Practice

We live in Miami and travel to the Virgin Islands. Becky Z. Fix prefers a quiet jet.

Digraph Practice (uz yf fm iy mc)

gauze joyful staffmen multiyear armchairs gauze joyful staffmen multiyear armchairs

97b ● **HA**
Evaluation ~ Analysis

Key the timed writing at the right.

Timed Writing

Nancy was able to enter the national spelling contest in Philadelphia for the second consecutive year. The first three words selected for her were armchairs, multiyear, and staffmen. The very next word she was asked was "gauze." She spelled that word correctly. Nancy was very joyful that she would be able to continue spelling. After about seven hours only twenty people remained. Only seven people remained at the end of the first day. Nancy won the national contest in Philadelphia on the second day.

97c Individualized Practice

Key the drill according to the prompts on your screen.

97d WordChamp

Play the game WordChamp.

97e End of Class Procedure . . .

if you are not continuing to the next Session.

Speed Clinic

The unused box of gauze was a puzzle to the five staffmen.

The multiyear celebration was a joyful event for all people.

They signed a multiyear contract to play in the South.

All staffmen were called to the main office to help work.

The beautiful leather armchair was placed by the window.

uz   gauze puzzle gauze puzzle gauze puzzle gauze puzzle gauze

yf   joyful joyful joyful joyful joyful joyful joyful joyful

fm   staffmen staffmen staffmen staffmen staffmen staffmen

iy   multiyear multiyear multiyear multiyear multiyear multiyear

mc   armchairs armchairs armchairs armchairs armchairs armchairs

Refer to page **R-1** for tips on efficient keying of individual letters.

Session 53—Skillbuilding

53a ●
Conditioning Practice

Key each exercise at the right three times.

Alphabetic Practice
Xavier B. Zayer was quite impressed by her knowledge of Japanese culture.

Digraph Practice (hu fl xe dg xi sf za lv)
hunt thus fly conflict boxes deluxe badge exist taxi satisfy zag pizzas solve

53b ● Ⓐ
Evaluation ~ Analysis

Key the timed writing at the right.

Timed Writing
The brochure that Elaine received when she was admitted to the business school briefly explained each of the required classes. She was very anxious to transfer to this new school as soon as she could. Elaine's resolve to exert all her efforts to advance her education should guarantee her success. She judged that a degree from a business school would be a sizable investment in her future.

53c Individualized Practice
Key the drill according to the prompts on your screen.

53d WordChamp
Play the game WordChamp.

53e End of Class Procedure . . .
if you are not continuing to the next Session.

Speed Clinic

Refer to page **R-1** for tips on efficient keying of individual letters.

Twelve huge pizzas came by taxicab. We were florists in the big city. I mixed the boxes of fudge. Angie was satisfied.

hu	hull huge human humble humor humid hunt thus shuffle sulphur
fl	flag flair flames flap flash florists rifle conflict leaflet
xe	boxed boxes exempt exercise exert taxed mixed relaxed deluxe
dg	wedge lodge badge dodge edge fudge ridge judge bridge pledge
xi	toxin exist exit toxic taxicab maximum fixing existing taxi
sf	transferred transformed satisfy transfer satisfied transform
za	zag hazard sizable pizzas hazards realization credenza plaza
lv	twelve solve silver halves involve valve dissolve silverware

Session 96—Skillbuilding

96a ●
Conditioning Practice
Key each exercise at the right three times.

Alphabetic Practice
Jacqueline and Zeb take daily walks. Running is one exciting form of physical activity.

Digraph Practice (yu gw lh uq)
yuletide wigwag silhouettes bouquet yuletide wigwag silhouettes bouquet yuletide wigwag silhouettes bouquet

---

96b ● **HA**
Evaluation ~ Analysis
Key the timed writing at the right.

Timed Writing
Peter was very excited as he anticipated the beginning of the second national spelling contest that was being held in one of his favorite cities, Philadelphia. The first four words selected for him were silhouettes, wigwag, bouquet, and yuletide. He was very happy; he was able to spell all four words correctly. The next word he was asked was very difficult; it was "banquets." Unfortunately, he misspelled that word.

96c Individualized Practice
Key the drill according to the prompts on your screen.

96d WordChamp
Play the game WordChamp.

96e End of Class Procedure . . .
if you are not continuing to the next Session.

Speed Clinic

This is the yuletide season. Everyone needs yuletide cheer.

To wigwag is to move back and forth. I saw them wigwag.

Which silhouette did you select from the many silhouettes?

She made a beautiful yuletide silhouette for their home site.

Where did you learn to wigwag like that? It takes work.

I saw the airplane silhouette in the distance. Look at them.

Did you send her a bouquet of roses? He sent two bouquets.

Refer to page R-1 for tips on efficient keying of individual letters.

yu   yuletide yuletide yuletide yuletide yuletide yuletide

gw   wigwag wigwag wigwag wigwag wigwag wigwag wigwag wigwag

lh   silhouettes silhouettes silhouettes silhouettes silhouettes

uq   bouquet bouquets bouquet bouquets bouquet bouquets bouquet

54a ●

Conditioning Practice

Key each exercise at the right three times.

Alphabetic Practice

Jack V. Quintin was first to realize the giant ax must always be sharpened.

Digraph Practice (yp yi sl ox dm)

bypass yield buying slim island oxygen toxic box admire admitted

---

54b ● **A**

Evaluation ~ Analysis

Key the timed writing at the right.

Timed Writing

The new school that Elaine was to attend, the Xavier Business College, required that one have typewriting skill prior to admission. She had extensive experience keying at her present job. She was very anxious to box up all of the items on her desk and leave her present job to pursue her education.

54c Individualized Practice

Key the drill according to the prompts on your screen.

54d WordChamp

Play the game WordChamp.

54e End of Class Procedure . . .

if you are not continuing to the next Session.

Speed Clinic

All grandmothers admire fast typists. Are you enjoying the island? How many boxes did you see her buying? The fox is in the box playing. There was little oxygen in the old box.

Lying in the sun and enjoying the surf was enjoyable to Sal.

What was the admission fee to sleep on the island last year?

Refer to page **R-1** for tips on efficient keying of individual letters.

yp   typist typing typical types type typed hypothesis typewriter

yi   yield yields buying crying enjoying lying playing destroying

sl   slacks slate sleep sleeve slice slim slum aisle island isles

ox   oxfords oxide oxygen proxy toxic boxes boxed paradox fox box

dm   grandmothers admire admission admitted admissions amendments

Session 95—Assessment

95a ●
Conditioning Practice
Key the exercise at the right three times.

Alphabetic Practices

Check a daily paper for a listing of available jobs. He and Suz will qualify by exam.

Van, Jan, and Felix saw two zebras grazing by a lake. Dale made a quick trip home.

Rachel, Vi, and Jeff went to the zoo to see chimps and a yak. Quint saw a big lynx.

Marney is our pet Westie, with white fur and jet black eyes. Vi quit the XYZ Dog Co.

95b ● Ⓐ
Evaluation ~ Progress
Key the first timed writing at the right.

95c ● Ⓐ
Evaluation ~ Progress
Key the second timed writing at the right.

95d ●
WordChamp
Play the game WordChamp.

95e ●
End of Class Procedure . . .
if you are not continuing to the next Session.

Speed Clinic

Emphasis: One-Hand Words

Timed Writing

Do you have a dictionary? Keep in mind that it is a very important tool. The dictionary can be a very useful guide for vocabulary improvement. A good dictionary gives many facts relative to words. For example, if you looked up the words fox, pizza, and jar, you would see that each word has its own set of information related to using the actual word. Every office should be equipped with a dictionary.

Timed Writing

Young people often experience difficulty in communicating with others because of their frequent use of slang. There is nothing wrong with slang, per se, but it is often difficult for others to understand the intended meaning. Can you make a list of the slang words you use and their intended meanings? Just keep it simple. Be ready to quiz your friends about the various meanings.

I'll trade you my sweater for your sweater. It's a good way to get him to trade. The bee stung her on the ear. What is the link between the vet and the cat? I'll get her an extra vest for the trip up the hill. What a joy to see them wed.

a joy bee lip cat mop dab nip ear on fad pin get up rag you

sat yolk tax ump vet ply we oil zest nil at my be link cards

knoll deer jimmy extra I'll few hill get him raw ion sweater

jolly trade kill vest lily wed milky zag ninny

Session 55—Assessment

55a ●
Conditioning Practice
Key the exercise at the right three times.

Alphabetic Practices
Jacob F. Lomax was very happy to know he got a good score on the quiz.

Paula F. Gabor liked very much to relax while enjoying quality jazz music.

Xavier B. Zayer was quite impressed by her knowledge of Japanese culture.

Jack V. Quintin was first to realize the giant ax must always be sharpened.

55b ● Ⓐ
Evaluation ~ Progress
Key the first timed writing at the right.

55c ● Ⓐ
Evaluation ~ Progress
Key the second timed writing at the right.

55d ●
WordChamp
Play the game WordChamp.

55e ●
End of Class Procedure . . .
if you are not continuing to the next Session.

Timed Writing
Any formula that will help you to choose a job wisely will be most valu-able. Your schooling, hobbies, experiences, traits, interests, ability, and health all enter into making a reasonable job choice. Keep in mind that while the list may be quite long, you must plan to capitalize on your strengths in each of the items.

Timed Writing
The laws of supply and demand have a great influence on both securing and keeping a job. If the supply of workers with specialized training is less than the demand, then the worker can be more selective in choosing a posi-tion. Of course, if the supply of workers exceeds the demand, a business can require much more from a prospective employee.

Speed Clinic

Left-Right Hand Drills

Millions see car races. Tag my vase for mom. The moon is a vast place. My mom and my dad have a monopoly. Dress for a debate. My puppy has a pink tag. The pup is only a year old.

I'll fax him a list of better brass beds. I fed a few cats.

races up raft upon rag union rage yip sad yolk safe you sags

sage you'll sat yolk save holly saved honk saves hook scared

tab hoop tact hop taffeta hulk tag hull tags hymn tarts loll

tar loon target mil tart mill taste million tax minimum tear

vacate millions vacates mink vase mom vases monopoly average

moon vast mop vat mull veer mum veered my verge nil verse no

Session 94 — Skillbuilding

94a ●
Conditioning Practice
Key each exercise at the right three times.

Alphabetic Practice
Marney is our pet Westie, with white fur and jet black eyes. Vi quit the XYZ Dog Co.

Digraph Practice (gd nz pk rq tz)
kingdom bronze credenza napkins upkeep torque blitz quartz

94b ● **HA**
Evaluation ~ Analysis
Key the timed writing at the right.

Timed Writing
    Larry said that only the very expensive torque necklace and quartz watches were on the credenza in their family room. The pieces of jewelry were purchased in the United Kingdom several decades ago. He placed all three pieces in a napkin for safekeeping until he had an opportunity to have them cleaned. Larry was very excited to be able to donate these three pieces of jewelry for charity.

94c Individualized Practice
Key the drill according to the prompts on your screen.

94d WordChamp
Play the game WordChamp.

94e End of Class Procedure ...
if you are not continuing to the next Session.

Speed Clinic

How many kingdoms did you read about in your history class?

The old item was made of bronze. What is quartz?

Look in my credenza for the package of white napkins also.

The upkeep was too much on his Florida condo. He sold it.

How much torque do you need to apply to install the motor?

gd	kingdom kingdom kingdom kingdom kingdom kingdom kingdom
nz	bronze credenza bronze credenza bronze credenza bronze
pk	napkins upkeep napkins upkeep napkins upkeep napkins upkeep
rq	torque torque torque torque torque torque torque torque
tz	blitz quartz blitz quartz blitz quartz blitz quartz blitz

Refer to page R-1 for tips on efficient keying of individual letters.

Session 56—Skillbuilding

56a ●
Conditioning Practice
Key each exercise at the right three times.

Alphabetic Practice
Madeline J. Fagan was very quick to realize the exact price of the bonus.

Digraph Practice (hy uf xa bt hs rf hl)
hybrid physics why bluff exact debts doubt withstand cloths surface wharf athletic

56b ● A
Evaluation ~ Analysis
Key the timed writing at the right.

Timed Writing
Did you know that every athlete must spend months performing very physical exercises in order to assure that his or her body is in top shape? To obtain the exact exercises best for you, you should always contact your own personal doctor. Don't be lazy; exercise is the stuff muscles are made of.

56c Individualized Practice
Key the drill according to the prompts on your screen.

56d WordChamp
Play the game WordChamp.

56e End of Class Procedure . . .
if you are not continuing to the next Session.

Speed Clinic

Why is the hydrant by the wharf off? She is athletic but we need to examine her. Why did they take baths? I doubt they suffer from monthly exams. Our curfew will be over soon.

hy	hybrid hydrant hydro hymn physics physician sympathy shy why
uf	bluff buff cuff puff scuff stuff suffer muffle luff sufferer
xa	taxable example exact exams exactly examine examples examine
bt	debts obtain subtract subtle debtor doubt redoubt doubt debt
hs	withstand notwithstanding lengths fifths oaths faiths baths
rf	wharf perfect fearful overflow overfull curfew perfect wharf
hl	athletic highly highlight monthly smoothly pamphlet highland

Refer to page R-1 for tips on efficient keying of individual letters.

Session 93—Skillbuilding

93a ●
Conditioning Practice
Key each exercise at the right three times.

Alphabetic Practice
Rachel, Vi, and Jeff went to the zoo to see chimps and a yak. Quint saw a big lynx.

Digraph Practice (fh fw mr mw)
offhand halfway comrade teamwork offhand halfway primrose teamwork

93b ●
Evaluation ~ Analysis
Key the timed writing at the right.

Timed Writing
Excellent high school athletes must have every one of the following characteristics: teamwork, comradeship, and honesty. Offhand, Vincent seemed to have all of these characteristics; and the new coach was very impressed with his basic ability. Halfway through the new season, the coach was very sure that many other members of the team, however, did not have many of them. A few members of the team entirely lacked every single trait.

93c Individualized Practice
Key the drill according to the prompts on your screen.

93d WordChamp
Play the game WordChamp.

93e End of Class Procedure . . .
if you are not continuing to the next Session.

Speed Clinic

The coach said that teamwork, teamwork, teamwork is the key.

Offhand I think my comrade needs to develop more teamwork.

They were led down the primrose lane by their old comrades.

Halfway to the city the team was told that teamwork is okay.

Stacey is my comrade. Suzanne is my comrade. So is Angie.

The beautiful plant was called a primrose. I liked them.

Refer to page **R-1** for tips on efficient keying of individual letters.

fh	offhand offhand offhand offhand offhand offhand offhand
fw	halfway halfway halfway halfway halfway halfway halfway
mr	comrade primrose comrade primrose comrade primrose comrade
mw	teamwork teamwork teamwork teamwork teamwork teamwork

57a ●
Conditioning Practice
Key each exercise at the right three times.

Alphabetic Practice
Mabel K. Virginia felt quite jinxed when she could not win any prize.

Digraph Practice (oe nm sw eh kl nq)
does foe abandonment swan answer behalf household booklet banquet

57b ● **A**
Evaluation ~ Analysis
Key the timed writing at the right.

Timed Writing
Inquire about all of the weekly exercise activities available in your own local area. When you have found a very rigorous program that you think meets all of your exact needs, you must then ask each of these questions: Does the sponsor stand behind every part of the program? Can you withstand the program rigor? Do the exercise assignments develop your muscles—and not just make you sweat?

57c Individualized Practice
Key the drill according to the prompts on your screen.

57d WordChamp
Play the game WordChamp.

57e End of Class Procedure . . .
if you are not continuing to the next Session.

Speed Clinic

Swap a sweater for a buckle. Hoe the potato patch. Inquire if the rehearsal is part of my classwork assignment. Behind the two vehicles is my new canoe. The checklist goes to our son. Take a weekly swim. The environment does matter also.

oe   does goes toes noel potatoes foe hoe canoe foe oboe toe shoe

nm   nonmembers unmatched unmarried assignment environment inmate

sw   sweater swap crosswise swell swim answer answering classwork

eh   behalf behavior behind rehearsal reheat vehicles dehydrating

kl   ankle booklet buckle checklist sparkle weekly trickle weekly

nq   banquet conquest inquire inquiry delinquent inquiry inquired

Refer to page **R-I** for tips on efficient keying of individual letters.

Session 92—Skillbuilding

92a ●
Conditioning Practice
Key each exercise at the right three times.

Alphabetic Practice
Van, Jan, and Felix saw two zebras grazing by a lake. Dale made a quick trip home.

Digraph Practice (mt sg vu wk dk)
warmth disgusted misgivings divulged revue awkward hawks handkerchief

92b ●
Evaluation ~ Analysis
Key the timed writing at the right.

Timed Writing
The Duke used his handkerchief to wipe his forehead. The warmth of the very, very hot day quickly caused the commander to change the schedule for many of the activities planned for later in the afternoon. The commander felt very awkward handling this important situation. His initial misgivings about divulging every detail of this assignment were correct.

92c Individualized Practice
Key the drill according to the prompts on your screen.

92d WordChamp
Play the game WordChamp.

92e End of Class Procedure . . .
if you are not continuing to the next Session.

Speed Clinic

In the warmth of the summer day he divulged the next secret.

They were disgusted and had misgivings about the new result.

I saw two large hawks on our golf course last Saturday.

It was awkward for them to hit the golf ball left-handed.

The officer divulged that the revue was held last weekend.

Nancy was given a beautiful handkerchief for her birthday.

mt   warmth warmth warmth warmth warmth warmth warmth warmth

sg   disgusted misgivings misguided disgusted misgiving

vu   divulged revue divulged revue divulged revue divulged revue

wk   awkward hawks awkward hawks awkward hawks awkward hawks hawk

dk   handkerchief handkerchiefs handkerchief handkerchiefs

Refer to page **R-1** for tips on efficient keying of individual letters.

Session 58 — Skillbuilding

58a ●
Conditioning Practice
Key each exercise at the right three times.

Alphabetic Practice
Alex V. Jacob was told he needed to go and buy a dozen quarts of milk.

Digraph Practice (bj iu lm oj rb wl)
object auditorium almanac realm project barber absorb knowledge bowl

---

58b ● Ⓐ
Evaluation ~ Analysis
Key the timed writing at the right.

Timed Writing

For almost fifty years, people in the United States have been slowly moving from rural to urban areas. This trend has been the subject of numerous studies. As more and more of the population moves, the radius of many cities is quickly expanding. It is projected that this trend will continue for many years to come. Very few people move from large urban areas to small rural areas.

58c Individualized Practice
Key the drill according to the prompts on your screen.

58d WordChamp
Play the game WordChamp.

58e End of Class Procedure . . .
if you are not continuing to the next Session.

Speed Clinic

The objective of the films was to show titanium golf clubs.

My barber is in the suburbs. Florida has palm trees. May I bowl at the new gymnasium? Projections for the new stadium are high. I saw an owl and waterfowl near the auditorium.

bj   object subject objected objection objective objects subjects

iu   triumph titanium stadium sodium medium gymnasium auditoriums

lm   almost elms films palmetto almanac films realm palm film elm

oj   project projected projection projector projects projections

rb   nearby carbon barber verbally absorb curb herb suburb superb

wl   bowls crawls slowly knowledge crawls waterfowl owl cowl bowl

Refer to page **R-1** for tips on efficient keying of individual letters.

Session 91—Skillbuilding

91a ●
Conditioning Practice
Key each exercise at the right three times.

Alphabetic Practice
Check a daily paper for a listing of available jobs. He and Suz will qualify by exam.

Digraph Practice (ih iw uk wc)
likelihood likelihood multiwall multiwall duke duke newcomer showcase

---

91b ● HA
Evaluation ~ Analysis
Key the timed writing at the right.

Timed Writing
    The new, multiwall complex was just built to provide additional security needed during the Duke's very first visit to their country. The security team realized that the likelihood of any problem was very small. The armed services showcased their new weapons as the Duke reviewed the very long parade. The parade was a great success!

91c Individualized Practice
Key the drill according to the prompts on your screen.

91d WordChamp
Play the game WordChamp.

91e End of Class Procedure . . .
if you are not continuing to the next Session.

Speed Clinic

The site was a showcase for the newcomer. Duke is my dog.

In all likelihood the new duke will arrive with his son.

They said that it was a multiwave event that hit us today.

The new unit will have a multiwall construction. I approve.

She was a newcomer to the newcomer's showcase party.

Do you like the name Duke? I think Duke is a fine name.

ih   likelihood likelihood likelihood likelihood likelihood

iw   multiwall multiwave multiwall multiwave multiwall multiwave

uk   duke duke duke duke duke duke duke duke duke duke duke duke

wc   newcomer newcomers showcase newcomer newcomers showcase

Refer to page R-1 for tips on efficient keying of individual letters.

Session 59—Skillbuilding

59a ●
Conditioning Practice
Key each exercise at the right three times.

Alphabetic Practice
Jack F. West realized he passed by the exit sign to Montana very quickly.

Digraph Practice (ix lk uo uy fy nj)
fixture affix talked milk quota buyer guy clarifying specify enjoyable

59b ● **A**
Evaluation ~ Analysis
Key the timed writing at the right.

Timed Writing
Many people realize they enjoy "cosmopolitan life." They can walk to a professional football match, take a taxicab to an auditorium to see a play, or buy food from a street vendor. Going to a city for the first time can leave you with mixed feelings. You may not be able to identify with the superfluous behavior of some professional people.

59c Individualized Practice
Key the drill according to the prompts on your screen.

59d WordChamp
Play the game WordChamp.

59e End of Class Procedure . . .
if you are not continuing to the next Session.

Speed Clinic

My folks are both sixty. Her quota is sixty quarts of milk.

Notify the buyer of the injury. Can I satisfy the guys with six silk shirts? She will testify at the injury trial soon.

Buyers will be buying based on quoted quotations on Tuesday.

Refer to page R-1 for tips on efficient keying of individual letters.

ix	sixth mixed fixing fixed sixty affix sixty fixed six mix fix
lk	folks talked walked walks silk bulk milk calk walk talk folk
uo	quoted quotas quote quota liquor quotation ingenuous arduous
uy	buys buyer buyers buying guys colloquy buy guy buyer buy guy
fy	satisfy modify fluffy testify notify signify certify glorify
nj	enjoy inject injure injury unjust enjoys injection enjoyment

90a •
Conditioning Practice
Key the exercise at the right three times.

Alphabetic Practices

Did Jim see Wyn unload the cargo of zircons? Barb removed six quality pieces for him to keep.

Gay ordered a sixteen oz. juicy rib eye steak for Paul. Helma wants a quality vintage wine.

Kim can realize a very rewarding and exciting job if she qualifies as a pilot.

When Jan Zelig bought a car for Felix Park, I questioned buying a very new model.

90b • A
Evaluation ~ Progress
Key the first timed writing at the right.

90c • A
Evaluation ~ Progress
Key the second timed writing at the right.

90d •
WordChamp
Play the game WordChamp.

90e •
End of Class Procedure . . .
if you are not continuing to the next Session.

Speed Clinic

Emphasis: Left-Hand Words

Timed Writing

Today, we have reached a summit in our search for perfection in illustrating our accounting records. Can you guess what device has made this possible? If you said the computer, you are right. The computer helps us organize our data, keeps track of our income and our expenses, and aids us in preparing our quarterly and yearly reports. It has made our job easier. Do you have one to help with your accounting records?

Timed Writing

The growing volume of paperwork in business has led to the use of some type of automation for most of the routine jobs, particularly in large offices. However, offices of all sizes are rapidly moving toward automation. Examine the amount of paper used in your company. Is the quantity consumed too much? What types of processing equipment do you have? Do you know how to use it? Who does the training?

Send them our regrets after their defeat at the sea regatta.
Do a good deed and receive the greatest reward. He can sew.
The sextet sang on a stage under the stars. It was great.
sew sewed sewer sews sextet stag stage star stare stars stew
refer refers regard regards regatta regret regrets reserves
grease great greater greatest greed greet greeted greats few
fewer free freed freezer freeze estate evade evaded exceeded
deed deeds deer defeat defeated defeats defer desert deserve
cedar crab craft crate crave craw craze crazed crease create

Session 60—Assessment

60a ●

Conditioning Practice

Key the exercise at the right three times.

Alphabetic Practices

Madeline J. Fagan was very quick to realize the exact price of the bonus.

Mabel K. Virginia felt quite jinxed when she could not win any prize.

Alex V. Jacob was told he needed to go and buy a dozen quarts of milk.

Jack F. West realized he passed by the exit sign to Montana very quickly.

60b ● Ⓐ

Evaluation ~ Progress

Key the first timed writing at the right.

60c ● Ⓐ

Evaluation ~ Progress

Key the second timed writing at the right.

60d ●

WordChamp

Play the game WordChamp.

60e ●

End of Class Procedure . . .

if you are not continuing to the next Session.

Timed Writing

The company organizational chart provides the means whereby a business firm is able to structure the lines of authority and define the division of work for each of its workers. Inquire about getting a chart from a local company. Have someone explain the chart to you. What jobs are shown?

Timed Writing

The letter of application gives a firm its first look at you as a potential worker. Details of this letter should be studied. Many an interview has ended before it has started due to poorly written letters. Before you write your first letter, you should acquaint yourself with the techniques of good letter writing. Be sure to examine and analyze several texts on the subject.

Speed Clinic

Left-Hand Words/ Right-Hand Words

At noon I had to add the abstract. The bear jumped over the brass bar. The batter lost his bat because of oily hands.

Go to the bazaar and get pink beads for our fall play. Tony had an opinion on the poll. They need a pompom for tonight.

a abstract abstracts access act acted acts ad adage add ages

ninny nip nook noon noun nul nun nylon oh ohm ho oil oily on

badger bar bare bars base based bass baste bat bats braggart

onion only opinion pill pin pink plink ploy plum plump polio

batter bazaar be bead beads bear bears beast beat beaver bed

plunk ply polio poll polo pomp pompom pony pooh pool pop pup

Session 89—Skillbuilding

89a ●
Conditioning Practice
Key each exercise at the right three times.

Alphabetic Practice
When Jan Zelig bought a car for Felix Park, I questioned buying a very new model.

Digraph Practice (ji bp bw gb)
jig jingling subparagraph bobwhite subway longboat springboard

89b ● HA
Evaluation ~ Analysis
Key the timed writing at the right.

Timed Writing
Kenneth Bogdanske heard the jingling of money in his trouser pocket as he quickly walked to the subway. During a very long train ride home, he had the opportunity to study subparagraph six of the entrants' contract he was required to sign before he would be given the opportunity to participate in the longboat contest.

89c Individualized Practice
Key the drill according to the prompts on your screen.

89d WordChamp
Play the game WordChamp.

89e End of Class Procedure . . .
if you are not continuing to the next Session.

Speed Clinic

A bobwhite is sometimes called a partridge. I see a bobwhite.

Go to subway exit ten to get the subway to your destination.

Did you see the longboat at the museum? What are longboats?

The game is a springboard to their next state championship.

Look for subparagraph four in the legal abstract. They did.

The jig was up. What is that jingling I hear in your hand?

ji   jig jingling jig jingling jig jingling jig jingling jingling

bp   subparagraph subparagraph subparagraph subparagraph

bw   bobwhite subway bobwhite subway bobwhite subway bobwhite

gb   longboat springboard longboat springboard longboat longboat

Refer to page R-1 for tips on efficient keying of individual letters.

Session 61—Skillbuilding

61a ●
Conditioning Practice
Key each exercise at the right three times.

Alphabetic Practice
Felix J. Clark realized the money for the gift plan would be quickly saved.

Digraph Practice (ya lr cs zi rh lw bb)
yacht loyalty already topics zinc analyzing rheumatic letterhead always abbey

61b ●
Evaluation ~ Analysis
Key the timed writing at the right.

Timed Writing
You may already know that both zinc and rhodium are very common metallic elements. Very often the study of elements such as these is one of the topics you must study in school. The subject is "chemistry," and you might not always find that it is enjoyable and exciting, or you might always rather pursue your favorite hobby.

61c Individualized Practice
Key the drill according to the prompts on your screen.

61d WordChamp
Play the game WordChamp.

61e End of Class Procedure . . .
if you are not continuing to the next Session.

Speed Clinic

I want to overhaul my yacht. What is your hobby? Perhaps I need to get my jewelry. It was freezing for the picnics. I always go by the railway on my way to the neighborhood.

ya   yacht yards yard yarn yarns loyalty royal loyal payable yard

lr   already railroad ballroom jewelry mailroom railroads already

cs   tactics plastics critics picnics ethics basics topics basics

zi   zig zinc zip zippers freezing magazine amazing zippy glazing

rh   rheumatic overhaul perhaps overhead letterhead neighborhood

lw   always hallway hallways millwork railway stalwart stalwarts

bb   abbey hobby lobby rabbit cabbage nibble robbery abbreviation

Refer to page R-1 for tips on efficient keying of individual letters.

Session 88—Skillbuilding

88a ●
Conditioning Practice
Key each exercise at the right three times.

Alphabetic Practice
Kim can realize a very rewarding and exciting job if she qualifies as a pilot.

Digraph Practice (wp xu df hp pc)
viewpoint cowpoke flexural luxury dreadful handful mothproof mouthpiece topcoat upcoming

88b ● HA
Evaluation ~ Analysis
Key the timed writing at the right.

Timed Writing
Jeffrey Reynolds didn't share his grandfather's viewpoint that a longboat was a luxury he could have done without. He just thought about how wonderful the opportunity of being a participant in the upcoming race would be. He realized he needed a mouthpiece to protect the new braces on his teeth from flying oars. He wanted every opportunity to become a skilled participant.

88c Individualized Practice
Key the drill according to the prompts on your screen.

88d WordChamp
Play the game WordChamp.

88e End of Class Procedure . . .
if you are not continuing to the next Session.

Speed Clinic

From the viewpoint of the cowpoke it was a good rodeo ride.

What is the meaning of flexural? Only a handful were here.

The grandfathers held steadfast to their demands to go to the upcoming game.

The player lost his mouthpiece before the final game began.

Should we mothproof the luxury cabinet? It was mothproofed.

wp cowpoke viewpoint viewpoints cowpoke viewpoint viewpoints

xu flexural luxury flexural luxury flexural luxury flexural

df dreadful grandfathers handful steadfastly grandfathers

hp mothproof mothproofed mouthpiece mothproof mothproofed

pc topcoats upcoming topcoats upcoming topcoats upcoming

Refer to page **R-1** for tips on efficient keying of individual letters.

62a •
Conditioning Practice

Key each exercise at the right three times.

Alphabetic Practice
George and Suzanne won seven tickets to the jazz festival. I had Quincy put them in my yellow box.

Digraph Practice (bm eb yt hw ka dj tc)
submarine ebony algebra web anything highway breakage eureka adjacent notch

62b • Ⓐ
Evaluation ~ Analysis

Key the timed writing at the right.

Timed Writing
Have you ever asked why you must study algebra in school? Will studying this subject help you in the future? It is remarkable how you can quickly adjust your attitude anytime you submerge yourself into a new topic that is of interest to you! Vary your interests. Don't be lazy! Just move along with dispatch every time a new challenge faces you. The outcome may surprise you.

62c Individualized Practice
Key the drill according to the prompts on your screen.

62d WordChamp
Play the game WordChamp.

62e End of Class Procedure . . .
if you are not continuing to the next Session.

Speed Clinic

Can you resubmit my request for the daytime debate? Anytime is okay for the submarine to submerge. Do I go northwest or southwest to find the highway? She adjusted the delivery of the package until it was repackaged by the packer.

bm	submit resubmit submarine submarines submerged resubmitting
eb	ebony debate debit rebate rebuilt debts debt rebuild neb web
yt	daytime anytime anything everything daytime anything anytime
hw	southwest highway northward highways northwest southwestern
ka	alkali workable okay workaday breakage package alkali eureka
dj	adjacent adjusted adjourn adjust readjust readjust adjourned
tc	notch botch catch catcher catchy etch etcetera fetch itch match

Refer to page **R-1** for tips on efficient keying of individual letters.

Session 87 — Skillbuilding

Refer to page R-1

87a ●
Conditioning Practice
Key each exercise at the right three times.

Alphabetic Practice
Gay ordered a sixteen oz. juicy rib eye steak for Paul. Helma wants a quality vintage wine.

Digraph Practice (ao pd kc kt)
chaos extraordinary update updated backcharge bookcase blacktop neckties

---

87b ● HA
Evaluation ~ Analysis
Key the timed writing at the right.

Timed Writing
Jack concluded that the entire construction process was in thorough chaos. The blacktop road leading to the aqueduct had not been completed. Backcharges had not been paid. The completed work did not reflect the updated plans. Jack concluded that it would be a major project to fix design errors and to finish work not completed.

- -

87c Individualized Practice
Key the drill according to the prompts on your screen.

87d WordChamp
Play the game WordChamp.

87e End of Class Procedure . . .
if you are not continuing to the next Session.

- -

Speed Clinic

The latest update said that it was chaos at the new site.

The bookcases were strewn all over the blacktop. I saw it.

The men must wear neckties to the cocktail party next week.

It was extraordinary that the crankcase did not crack.

They gave frequent updates on the accident. When will they give the next updated report? Look up the word backcharge.

Refer to page R-1 for tips on efficient keying of individual letters.

ao   chaos extraordinary chaos extraordinary chaos extraordinary

pd   update updated updates updating update updated updates

kc   backcharge bookcases backcharge crankcase bookcases

kt   blacktop cocktail cocktails neckties blacktop cocktails

Session 63 — Skillbuilding

63a ●
Conditioning Practice
Key each exercise at the right three times.

Alphabetic Practice
Gilbert asked the band to play a fox trot. Wally was amazed when Bev and Jack became quiet.

Digraph Practice (tg aj hn hm cq iq dn)
mortgage majestic technical freshman acquaint liquid goodness

---

63b ● Ⓐ
Evaluation ~ Analysis
Key the timed writing at the right.

Timed Writing
Keep in mind that buying a home represents a major acquisition. You must apply for a mortgage, and you must understand all the technical language involved. You shouldn't have too many debts and should have enough liquid assets to provide enough cash for the down payment. Don't make this task seem like punishment!

63c Individualized Practice
Key the drill according to the prompts on your screen.

63d WordChamp
Play the game WordChamp.

63e End of Class Procedure . . .
if you are not continuing to the next Session.

Speed Clinic

Didn't you meet my freshman acquaintance? He is majoring in technology. I have a unique understanding of arithmetic. I have a major mortgage. The majority do not have asthma.

Refer to page R-1 for tips on efficient keying of individual letters.

tg	mortgage mortgages mortgaged mortgagee mortgagors mortgagees
aj	major majors majestic majoring majority pajamas major majors
hn	doughnuts technical technique technology technician technic
hm	asthma freshman punishment attachment arithmetic attachments
cq	acquaint acquaintance acquainted acquired acquire acquainted
iq	unique antique liquid piqued liquor liquids uniquely liquids
dn	couldn't didn't hadn't shouldn't midnight sadness kindnesses

86a ●

Conditioning Practice

Key each exercise at the right three times.

Alphabetic Practice

Did Jim see Wyn unload the cargo of zircons? Barb removed six quality pieces for him to keep.

Digraph Practice (ii pb aq kr pg)

skiing clipboard cupboard aqueduct plaque bankrupt buckram stopgap upgrade

86b ● HA

Evaluation ~ Analysis

Key the timed writing at the right.

Timed Writing

Jack Zimmerman made notes on his clipboard while walking along the aqueduct. The firm that built the aqueduct went bankrupt; many individuals felt that the construction work would have to be upgraded to assure safety. While checking the quality of the work, he saw an individual skiing on the river below.

86c Individualized Practice

Key the drill according to the prompts on your screen.

86d WordChamp

Play the game WordChamp.

86e End of Class Procedure . . .

if you are not continuing to the next Session.

Speed Clinic

Refer to page R-1 for tips on efficient keying of individual letters.

The chipboard was near the cupboard. I need two clipboards.

The old city has many aqueducts. Look up the word aqueduct.

The dentist said that Nicholas had a plaque problem as well.

If you are bankrupt you must go to bankruptcy court.

Do you wish to upgrade your skiing equipment before you go?

ii   skiing skiing skiing skiing skiing skiing skiing skiing

pb   chipboard cupboard chipboard clipboard chipboard clipboard

aq   aqueducts plaque plaques vaquero aqueducts plaque plaques

kr   bankrupt bankruptcy buckram bankrupt bankruptcy bankrupt

pg   stopgap upgrade upgraded upgrading stopgap upgrade upgraded

Session 64 — Skillbuilding

64a ●
Conditioning Practice
Key each exercise at the right three times.

Alphabetic Practice

Should the quotations be itemized according to their weekly invoices? Just ask Rex and Pat first.

Digraph Practice (lc az tf yl pf eu)

welcomes amaze delightful cylinder helpful eureka amateur lieu

---

64b ● Ⓐ
Evaluation ~ Analysis
Key the timed writing at the right.

Timed Writing

Realize that you are responsible for calculating the cost of purchasing a home. Using tables provided by real estate agents will be helpful; you will be amazed. You will quickly discover that this purchase should not be left to an amateur. Select a good agent because it is doubtful that you will be able to find the style home you want by yourself.

64c Individualized Practice
Key the drill according to the prompts on your screen.

64d WordChamp
Play the game WordChamp.

64e End of Class Procedure . . .
if you are not continuing to the next Session.

Speed Clinic

You can be helpful and pick out a nylon outfit. I must give the museum a welcome call for my reunion. Their lieutenant was welcome at the reunion. Nylons are very stylish today.

He was amazed at how lazy the lieutenant was at the museum.

lc   welcome ulcer mulch calcium balcony calculus calculate ulcer

az   maze amaze amazed gaze gazing hazard hazards lazy amazingly

tf   outfit outfits rightful hurtful platform thoughtful doubtful

yl   nylon style bylaw nylons bylaws daylight stylish wryly vinyl

pf   helpful helpfully helpfulness helpful helpfully helpfulness

eu   eureka amateur lieutenant makeup museum reunion reusing lieu

Refer to page **R-1** for tips on efficient keying of individual letters.

Session 85—Assessment

85a ●
Conditioning Practice
Key the exercise at the right three times.

Alphabetic Practices

Find Austria, New Zealand, and the Falklands on my map. Vi, Toby, and Jack got an extra quiz.

Wynn and Van plan to be prepared for the major quiz. Can I ask Gil for help with the texts?

My records need to be examined by quality experts. Jack and Zack will be on flight seven.

Take Felix to the airport before the plane departs. Jan Zyg was very calm and quiet.

85b ●
Evaluation ~ Progress
Key the first timed writing at the right.

85c ● A
Evaluation ~ Progress
Key the second timed writing at the right.

Timed Writing

Writing is an important means of communication, for it provides a permanent record. In all communication, two factors need to be considered: speed and accuracy. On your job how much writing do you do? Do you keep an appointment book for notes? Quiz yourself on these points the next time you have to prepare a document.

85d ●
WordChamp
Play the game WordChamp.

85e ●
End of Class Procedure . . .
if you are not continuing to the next Session.

Timed Writing

The good business letter is simple and gets right to the point. It should convey its message as briefly as possible without giving up its completeness. Critique a business letter from one of your files. Examine the letter for brevity. Did the writer keep it simple? Jot down anything else you feel needs to be analyzed.

One-Hand Words
Two lines of left- and one line of right-hand words.

Do not use a nylon cord on your pup. My pup and cat have no access to the hill area near my home. They were awarded our pin for art appreciation. Plan to debate the class at noon.

I asked for no onion on my burger. Meet the nun at the inn.

area areas art arts as access ate average averaged averages

carves case cases cast cat cater cats cave caves caw ceased

hull hulk hook hop holly honk hip hill him ill inn in ink in

cease dear debate debt debts decrease decreased decreases

avert award awarded awards aware awl ax cars carve carved

pup pulp pink pin pun oh ho oil only onion no noon nun nylon

65a ●
Conditioning Practice

Key the exercise at the right three times.

Alphabetic Practices

Felix J. Clark realized the money for the gift plan would be quickly saved.

George and Suzanne won seven tickets to the jazz festival. I had Quincy put them in my yellow box.

Gilbert asked the band to play a fox trot. Wally was amazed when Bev and Jack became quiet.

Should the quotations be itemized according to their weekly invoices? Just ask Rex and Pat first.

65b ● Ⓐ
Evaluation ~ Progress

Key the first timed writing at the right.

65c ● Ⓐ
Evaluation ~ Progress

Key the second timed writing at the right.

65d ●
WordChamp

Play the game WordChamp.

65e ●
End of Class Procedure . . .

if you are not continuing to the next Session.

Speed Clinic

Left-Hand Words/ Right-Hand Words

Timed Writing

Businesses measure a job seeker using several means, including an interview, grades and records, skill and aptitude testing, and references. During a job inteview with you, an interviewer will look for traits that may quickly show the way you will act on the job. It is important that you zero in on those experiences that will make you look good. Plan to be at your best for your job interview.

Timed Writing

You should be aware of the fact that energy, alertness, and education can be stepping stones from a beginning job to more significant opportunities in your company. Those workers who learn quickly on the job move up in both title and salary. Do you have the expertise to advance? What skills do you presently have that you can utilize to your best advantage?

Beware of the braggart. The beggars begged to see the beef.

Jimmy was a kin of the old beggar. Do not pull the pup that way. I bet you'll join the team known as the Braves today.

She is a great yo-yo player. They did the task in a breeze.

beds bee bees beef beet beets beg beggar begged begs breezes

poplin poppy pull pulp pulpy pump pun punk puny pup pupil on

best bet bets better beware brace braced braces brag bragged

puppy yip yolk yon you you'll yo-yo up upon union ump ill ink

braggart brass brave braved braves breeze breezes bad bag at

jimmy jink join jolly joy junk kill kiln kilo kimono kin lip

84a ●
Conditioning Practice

Key each exercise at the right three times.

Alphabetic Practice
Take Felix to the airport before the plane departs. Jan Zyg was very calm and quiet.

Digraph Practice (hq uu wb)
earthquake vacuum drawback strawberry earthquake vacuum

84b ● (HA)
Evaluation ~ Analysis

Key the timed writing at the right.

Timed Writing
Gerry had never gone to the annual company picnic since she moved here but always stayed home doing her spring cleaning. While vacuuming, she could feel the very slightest rumble of a minor earthquake. Very scared, but not injured, she felt this was only a very small drawback. There were many advantages to living in California.

84c Individualized Practice
Key the drill according to the prompts on your screen.

84d WordChamp
Play the game WordChamp.

84e End of Class Procedure . . .
if you are not continuing to the next Session.

Speed Clinic

Refer to page **R-I** for tips on efficient keying of individual letters.

We lost all our rowboats in the last major earthquake. Can you vacuum the livingroom before I get home? Fifty rowboats were in the strawberry festival last year. Was it a serious drawback to have the old cowboys ride with the young cowboy?

The cowboy delivered the newborn calf. Vacuum tubes are not used in computers today. Earthquakes can happen anywhere in the world. Strawberry is a favorite soda flavor for the new cowboys.

hq   earthquake earthquakes earthquake earthquakes earthquake

uu   vacuum vacuums vacuum vacuums vacuum vacuums vacuum vacuums

wb   cowboy drawback newborn rowboats strawberry cowboy rowboats

66a ●
Conditioning Practice
Key each exercise at the right three times.

Alphabetic Practice
The spelling list contained the following words: empty, bought, quick, jazz, convex.

Digraph Practice (nr gt sn gy ah mn yr vy)
enrich length snapshot carelessness gypsum argyle biology ahead mahogany yeah alumni column payroll envy

66b ● (A)
Evaluation ~ Analysis
Key the timed writing at the right.

Timed Writing
Not all people will be able to define these words: argyle, copyright, mahogany, and alumni. You might even envy those people who can define them. Since it doesn't take much time for you to just look up a word in a dictionary, strengthen your vocabulary by looking up every new word you don't know. Remember, you can enrich your life by additional knowledge. Learn to use a dictionary.

66c Individualized Practice
Key the drill according to the prompts on your screen.

66d WordChamp
Play the game WordChamp.

66e End of Class Procedure . . .
if you are not continuing to the next Session.

Speed Clinic

Refer to page **R-1** for tips on efficient keying of individual letters.

The ivy was covered by snowfall the length of the gym. Most alumni are on the navy payroll. Enroll ahead of springtime.

nr   enroll unrest inroads enrich enroute unrelated unrest unruly

gt   length lengths strength strengthen strengths lengthen length

sn   snack snap sneak snow snacks snappy snapshot snowed snowfall

gy   gym gymnasium apology biology buggy clergy energy psychology

ah   ahead mahogany yeah ahead mahogany yeah ahead mahogany yeah

mn   alumni columnist columns hymns gymnastics hymn autumn column

yr   syrup payroll pyramid playrooms copyright styrene skyrockets

vy   envy navy heavy ivy levy envy navy heavy ivy levy heavy envy

Session 83 — Skillbuilding

83a ●
Conditioning Practice
Key each exercise at the right three times.

Alphabetic Practice
My records need to be examined by quality experts. Jack and Zack will be on flight seven.

Digraph Practice (pw cn bn pn wf zl)
shopworn picnic abnormal dampness lawfully puzzle

83b ● (HA)
Evaluation ~ Analysis
Key the timed writing at the right.

Timed Writing
The temperature this year was abnormally high during the annual company picnic. Just shortly after noon, it moved upward to just under a very sizzling one hundred degrees. The temperature was simply awful! People could feel the dampness in their clothing caused by the excessive heat, and many wanted relief. Many people felt the company should schedule the picnic during a different month every year.

83c Individualized Practice
Key the drill according to the prompts on your screen.

83d WordChamp
Play the game WordChamp.

83e End of Class Procedure . . .
if you are not continuing to the next Session.

Speed Clinic

Did you ever go picnicking after a snowfall? They might get pneumonia from the dampness. The abnormalities are puzzling to our doctor. Upwards of fifty persons tried to solve this puzzle. But no one was equipped to fix the shopworn tools.

pw   shopworn topwork topworking upward upwards shopworn topwork

cn   picnic picnicking picnics picnic picnicking picnics picnic

bn   abnormal abnormalities abnormally abnormal abnormalities

pn   dampness pneumatic pneumonia dampness pneumatic pneumonia

wf   awful awfully lawfully snowfall unlawful awful awfully awful

zl   nozzle nozzles puzzle puzzled puzzling sizzling puzzling

Refer to page **R-1** for tips on efficient keying of individual letters.

67a ●
Conditioning Practice
Key each exercise at the right three times.

Alphabetic Practice
The instructor asked Jim to define the following: behavior, jazz, valor, proxy, quota.

Digraph Practice (oz wt np fs gm)
dozen growth commonplace offspring beliefs acknowledgment segment

67b ● Ⓐ
Evaluation ~ Analysis
Key the timed writing at the right.

Timed Writing
People with very poor vocabularies are commonplace in the United States. In order to experience growth in their vocabulary, some people make sure that they learn a minimum of a dozen new words each year. There is a stigma attached to people with weak vocabularies, and it is not easy to offset this problem. Never quit learning; set a minimum goal of learning a new word each week.

67c Individualized Practice
Key the drill according to the prompts on your screen.

67d WordChamp
Play the game WordChamp.

67e End of Class Procedure . . .
if you are not continuing to the next Session.

Speed Clinic

We do not have the manpower for the bulldozers. Tariffs are unpaid because of layoffs. Growth in manpower will augment the layoffs. In my judgment the dozen nozzles are frozen.

Unpack the frozen nozzles. Fragments from the damaged roof fell on the bulldozer. In their judgment growth will come.

oz frozen dozens dozen nozzle bulldozer nozzles bulldozer dozen

wt growth growth growth growth growth growth growth growth

np input unpack tinplate unpaid unproven manpower unpredictable

fs offset offspring beliefs layoffs proofs roofs briefs tariffs

gm fragments judgment segment augment pigment fragments augment

Refer to page **R-1** for tips on efficient keying of individual letters.

Session 82—Skillbuilding

82a ●
Conditioning Practice

Key each exercise at the right three times.

Alphabetic Practice

Wynn and Van plan to be prepared for the major quiz. Can I ask Gil for help with the texts?

Digraph Practice (yg kw ko)

hygiene playground awkward walkways hickory kickoff

82b ● HA
Evaluation ~ Analysis

Key the timed writing at the right.

Timed Writing

While every adult member of the community worked very quickly to stop the flood danger, children could be seen sunbathing on the playground. An individual of the community was assigned to be a lookout to assure that children were never placed in danger. It just seemed awkward and unbelievable to watch children play while individual adult residents worked very hard maneuvering to avoid a flood.

82c Individualized Practice

Key the drill according to the prompts on your screen.

82d WordChamp

Play the game WordChamp.

82e End of Class Procedure . . .

if you are not continuing to the next Session.

Speed Clinic

Refer to page **R-1** for tips on efficient keying of individual letters.

Hygiene is very important if you want to be on a playground.

The lookout had a large spyglass to check the large islands.

I need to refill my oxygen bottle before they resume diving.

The ship's crew appeared like clockwork. It was awkward.

What does the word pekoe mean to you? Is it a type of tea?

Look for the lookout by the hickory tree on the island.

yg   hygiene oxygen playground spyglass hygiene oxygen playground

kw   awkward backward backwards backwork clockwise clockwork

ko   hickory kickoff knockouts lookout pekoe walkouts knockouts

Session 68 — Skillbuilding

68a ●
Conditioning Practice
Key each exercise at the right three times.

Alphabetic Practice

What do you think of these names for a baby: Jonah, Xavier, Calypso? Pick a dozen good ones quickly.

Digraph Practice (dw xh mf tn yw hb)

dwelling midway exhaust comfortable correctness anyway neighborhood

---

68b ● Ⓐ
Evaluation ~ Analysis
Key the timed writing at the right.

Timed Writing

Anyone who works at a computer terminal all day knows that it can be quite exhausting and can cause a lot of discomfort. Recently, many companies have begun to consider the PC user and are making hardware purchases with the physical fitness of the user in mind. You can see these changes everywhere. The comfort of everyone in the company from the person who runs the switchboard to the president should be considered when any equipment purchases are made.

68c Individualized Practice
Key the drill according to the prompts on your screen.

68d WordChamp
Play the game WordChamp.

68e End of Class Procedure . . .
if you are not continuing to the next Session.

Speed Clinic

Midway through midwinter the witness saw lightning in their neighborhood. The lightning was everywhere. Neighbors may exhibit goodwill by doing good deeds. I had discomfort when I fell last winter. It was a comfortable midweek at home.

Refer to page R-1 for tips on efficient keying of individual letters.

dw	hardware midweek broadway goodwill midwinter midway woodwork
xh	exhaust exhibit exhibits exhaustive exhibited exhaustive
mf	comfort comfortable comfortably comforts discomfort comforts
tn	lightning witness promptness fitness partner witness partner
yw	anyway anywhere everywhere haywire plywood anyway everywhere
hb	neighbor neighborhood neighbors switchboard thoroughbred

Session *81*—Skillbuilding

81a ●
Conditioning Practice
Key each exercise at the right three times.

Alphabetic Practice
Find Austria, New Zealand, and the Falklands on my map. Vi, Toby, and Jack got an extra quiz.

Digraph Practice (kp zz gf uv nb xl)
bookplate nozzle meaningful juvenile unbelievable axle

81b ● HA
Evaluation ~ Analysis
Key the timed writing at the right.

Timed Writing
Edward very quickly stockpiled sandbags in the sizzling sun. Company after company located in the community permitted many supervisors and workers to assist in the meaningful community effort. Workers loaded a truck with so many bags of sand that one of the axles was broken. Many of the residents felt that it was unbelievable that they could have a flood. The amount of assistance was simply wonderful! Would the maneuvering stop the water?

81c Individualized Practice
Key the drill according to the prompts on your screen.

81d WordChamp
Play the game WordChamp.

81e End of Class Procedure . . .
if you are not continuing to the next Session.

Speed Clinic

Do we need to stockpile all those axles? You can't maneuver with a broken axle. Sunbathing is great in Florida. Pizzas are the prize for the inbound air crew. They tried to have a meaningful relationship last year.

kp   bookplate bookplates stockpile stockpiled stockpiles

zz   nozzle nozzles pizza pizzas puzzle puzzled puzzling sizzling

gf   meaningful wrongful meaningful wrongful meaningful wrongful

uv   juvenile juveniles maneuver maneuvered maneuvering souvenir

nb   inboard inbound sunbathing unbalanced unbeatable unbiased

xl   axle axles axle axles axle axles axle axles axle axles axle

Refer to page **R-1** for tips on efficient keying of individual letters.

Session 69 — Skillbuilding

69a •
Conditioning Practice
Key each exercise at the right three times.

Alphabetic Practice
Ben wants Zack to develop my list of retirement goals. Can I expect Quincy to justify his position?

Digraph Practice (nw sq kg ln hd yc zo)
meanwhile squares esquire background illness kiln birthday boycott zone horizon

69b • Ⓐ
Evaluation ~ Analysis
Key the timed writing at the right.

Timed Writing
Large organizations are squarely on the cutting edge of new technology. They study the usefulness of new software on the horizon because they know it would be unwise to withdraw and let technology pass them by. When you work for a company, you can't work just for a paycheck. You must apply new technology whenever possible and keep up with it to maintain the background necessary for your job.

69c Individualized Practice
Key the drill according to the prompts on your screen.

69d WordChamp
Play the game WordChamp.

69e End of Class Procedure . . .
if you are not continuing to the next Session.

Speed Clinic

For my birthday I got a motorcycle. Unwrap the presents. I saw a squirrel in the background. I gave a walnut to Angela to give to the squirrel at the petting zoo. He won a razor.

nw   unwrap unwise unwanted unwelcome meanwhile nationwide unwrap

sq   squirt squeeze square squirrel squaw squad esquire squarely

kg   background backgrounds backguard background backgrounds

ln   walnut illness usefulness thoughtfulness helpfulness kiln

hd   birthday withdraw withdrawal withdrawn withdraws withdrawing

yc   boycott cycle cycles cyclones paycheck motorcycle psychology

zo   zone zoned zones zoning zooming zoos razor horizon horizons

Refer to page R-1 for tips on efficient keying of individual letters.

80a ●
Conditioning Practice
Key the exercise at the right three times.

Alphabetic Practices

Zane asked what is the purpose of an interview. Bill can just go quickly to the exam.

What does your boss need to know about Gwynn? Please fix a very cold quart of milk for Jill Zorn.

Your boss must be favorably impressed to offer Jack Waxman a job. Did Gil organize his critique?

Kim and Zelda would like to take accounting first. They plan on giving help to BJ Quinn next.

80b ●
Evaluation ~ Progress
Key the first timed writing at the right.

80c ●
Evaluation ~ Progress
Key the second timed writing at the right.

80d ●
WordChamp
Play the game WordChamp.

80e ●
End of Class Procedure . . .
if you are not continuing to the next Session.

Speed Clinic

Timed Writing

Teamwork is a very important concept. It is not unique to any one aspect of our lives. It can be developed in both the sports world and in the business world. The concept is developed through cooperation. It does not happen by itself. It grows through both individual and group participation. Just consider what excellent teamwork leads to in the sports arena. The same prize can be won in business.

Timed Writing

The higher you climb the employment ladder, the more thoroughly you must plan your preparation. Opportunities for men and women are greater now than ever before. However, the competition is keen, and the one who can do the job best is the one who will advance more rapidly. Learn your skills to qualify and expect to claim the advancement prize.

Wax the car for my date. I'll have a carafe of coffee and a couple of eggs. The computer erased my dated data and left me in a daze. After I waxed my car I met them at the career center. This is a new era. They plan to work faster.

wax wed wag warts waxed weed wage was waxes weeds wages were

we add ads affect after age ages agree agreed agrees arc are

cages car carafe card cards care cared career careers carets

cares caret data date dated dates daze dazed dead deaf debts

edge edges effect effects egg eggs era erase erased extracts

faster faze fazed fear fears feat fed fee feed fees feet few

70a •
Conditioning Practice
Key the exercise at the right three times.

Alphabetic Practices

The spelling list contained the following words: empty, bought, quick, jazz, convex.

The instructor asked Jim to define the following: behavior, jazz, valor, proxy, quota.

What do you think of these names for a baby: Jonah, Xavier, Calypso? Pick a dozen good ones quickly.

Ben wants Zack to develop my list of retirement goals. Can I expect Quincy to justify his position?

70b • (A)
Evaluation ~ Progress
Key the first timed writing at the right.

70c • (A)
Evaluation ~ Progress
Key the second timed writing at the right.

70d •
WordChamp
Play the game WordChamp.

70e •
End of Class Procedure . . .
if you are not continuing to the next Session.

Speed Clinic

Left-Hand Words

Timed Writing

When you examine the list of personality traits important to job success, you will recognize the trait of enthusiasm. This trait is important for your success on the job. A good, positive work attitude includes enthusiasm, both for the work and for the company. In your quest for job success, please keep in mind that this trait can be contagious.

Timed Writing

Finding enjoyable and suitable work is not a simple matter. Many people only discover their liking or disliking for different kinds of jobs after they have been working for months or even years. You should begin to prepare a list of careers you might like to have. Recognize and expect changes to your career list. Also inquire as to what is required at the entry level for each job.

Did you see the zebras zigzag through the water? He should have a vest on if they are going rafting. The ragweed count is very high this year. At this rate my taxes will be high.

Let's meet them on the first tee. I need a tee to test this new golf ball. She had tears when she saw the still sea.

zag zebra zebras zed zest wad war water wear west wade weave

verse vest vet vex vexed taxed taxes tea tears tee test tact

sag saw saws sax scare scarf scatter screw sea sear see star

rags ragweed rare rat rate rated rates rave raw raze readers

gaff gate gave gaze gazed gazes gear geese get gets fad fade

Session 79—Skillbuilding

79a ●
Conditioning Practice
Key each exercise at the right three times.

Alphabetic Practice
Kim and Zelda would like to take accounting first. They plan on giving help to BJ Quinn next.

Digraph Practice (xy td kb kk wd)
oxygen epoxy outdated checkbook bookkeeper overcrowded

79b ●
Evaluation ~ Analysis
Key the timed writing at the right.

Timed Writing

Frank Quale didn't make it to the annual meeting of stockholders; he authorized the bookkeeper of his company to cast his specific votes by proxy. The policies decided by the stockholders at this very crowded meeting will form the backbone of the company. The participants felt it was time to eliminate many outdated policies.

79c Individualized Practice
Key the drill according to the prompts on your screen.

79d WordChamp
Play the game WordChamp.

79e End of Class Procedure . . .
if you are not continuing to the next Session.

Speed Clinic

Overcrowding in a close area can cause loss of oxygen. They feel the bookkeeper will shutdown the outdoor theaters. May I see your checkbook? The bookkeeper had an outdated proxy.

Do you like the outdoors? We used an epoxy cement to glue a broken vase. Did anyone in the crowd have any backbone?

xy	epoxy oxygen proxy epoxy oxygen proxy epoxy oxygen proxy
td	outdated shutdown outdo outdoor outdoors outdated outdoor
kb	backbone brickbats checkbook workbook backbone checkbooks
kk	bookkeeper bookkeepers bookkeeping bookkeeper bookkeepers
wd	crowd crowded howdy overcrowded overcrowding powder powdered

Refer to page **R-1** for tips on efficient keying of individual letters.

71a ●
Conditioning Practice
Key each exercise at the right three times.

Alphabetic Practice
Does Jarvis know the zip code for Albuquerque, New Mexico? Yes, and I think Grover does too.

Digraph Practice (nx bv yb yh lb sb km)
anxiety obvious anybody policyholder sailboat bulb disburse workmanship

71b ● Ⓐ
Evaluation ~ Analysis
Key the timed writing at the right.

Timed Writing

The anxiety of the high school football team was very obvious to anybody who met any of the members. The Greyhound bus would be adjacent to the high school to take them to the championship. A victory today means a state title. Support was outstanding. The whole town was behind them; workmen had put up billboards and had disbursed flyers all over town asking for support.

71c Individualized Practice
Key the drill according to the prompts on your screen.

71d WordChamp
Play the game WordChamp.

71e End of Class Procedure . . .
if you are not continuing to the next Session.

Speed Clinic

My husband was anxious to see a sailboat. Obviously Ted may be a playboy. The workman found my passbook. Policyholders and everybody else can have an album. Check their keyboard.

nx   anxiety anxious anxiously anxiety anxious anxiously anxious

bv   obviate obvious obviously subversion obviate obvious obviate

yb   anybody everybody hybrid keyboard maybe playboy storyboards

yh   boyhood greyhound policyholder policyholders policyholders

lb   album albums billboard bulbs sailboat rollback sailboat bulb

sb   husbands passbook asbestos disburse disbursement pressboard

km   milkman stockmen workmen embankment workmanship workmanlike

Refer to page R-1 for tips on efficient keying of individual letters.

78a ●
Conditioning Practice
Key each exercise at the right three times.

Alphabetic Practice
Your boss must be favorably impressed to offer Jack Waxman a job. Did Gil organize his critique?

Digraph Practice (wm hf yn dh lg)
endowment faithful keynote adherence indulgence

78b ● HA
Evaluation ~ Analysis
Key the timed writing at the right.

Timed Writing
Zelda Carter was very quick to refuse to divulge the donor of the very large endowment her company had just received. As keynote speaker at the bondholders meeting, she did not feel that the meeting was an appropriate time to provide this very confidential information. In addition, she was very careful to remain faithful to the contributor who asked the company to keep the information anonymous.

78c Individualized Practice
Key the drill according to the prompts on your screen.

78d WordChamp
Play the game WordChamp.

78e End of Class Procedure . . .
if you are not continuing to the next Session.

Speed Clinic

All the faithful graduates were at the endowment ceremony.

My childhood friend divulged the contents of the fellowship.

You are the next keynote speaker. Please adhere to all the rules. Algebra is my worst subject. It's wishful thinking to expect bondholders to adhere to all those new rules.

Refer to page **R-1** for tips on efficient keying of individual letters.

wm	endowment endowments fellowman sawmill endowment fellowman
hf	faithful mouthful youthful wishful healthful healthfulness
yn	dynamic syndicate synthetics dynamics keynote lynch keynote
dh	adhere adhered adherence adherent adheres adhesive childhood
lg	algebra bulge indulge indulgence bulging divulged promulgate

72a •
Conditioning Practice
Key each exercise at the right three times.

Alphabetic Practice
Which of the following have the letter c in the word: zing, physics, but, exquisite, hawk, jam?

Digraph Practice (ja dq tb sr nh yd)
jargon adjacent headquarters basketball classroom enhance everyday

72b • Ⓐ
Evaluation ~ Analysis
Key the timed writing at the right.

Timed Writing

The city football team could not have worked any harder to win the title than they did this week: they all practiced very hard every day after school to learn many new plays; they all completed the many required classroom activities; and they all worked three or more days this week at the gym to enhance and develop their individual physical strength. They all realize that if they can only win today, their football team will have earned a trip to the headquarters of the national high school football association in New York City in January.

72c Individualized Practice
Key the drill according to the prompts on your screen.

72d WordChamp
Play the game WordChamp.

72e End of Class Procedure . . .
if you are not continuing to the next Session.

Speed Clinic

Basketball jackets are in the classroom. My inheritance was shown on the newsreel. The hydro plant needs a janitor. We went to our headquarters on payday. Can Stacy play softball or football everyday? There was a disruption in the class.

ja   jargon pajamas jar jaws jail jacket jars janitor jacks jars

dq   headquarters headquarters headquarters headquarters

tb   basketball football softball textbook outbreak pocketbooks

sr   classroom disregard disrespect disruption newsreel misrule

nh   unhappy unheard enhance downhill inheritance unhesitatingly

yd   everyday hydrant payday hydrogen dehydrated hydraulic hydro

Refer to page R-1 for tips on efficient keying of individual letters.

Session 77 — Skillbuilding

Refer to page R-I for tips on efficient keying of individual letters.

77a ●
Conditioning Practice
Key each exercise at the right three times.

Alphabetic Practice

What does your boss need to know about Gwynn? Please fix a very cold quart of milk for Jill Zorn.

Digraph Practice (ae dp hh sd)

aerobic anaesthesia larvae grandparents withheld jurisdiction

77b ● HA
Evaluation ~ Analysis
Key the timed writing at the right.

Timed Writing

Use considerable wisdom when you decide to participate in an aerobics program. You should always withhold very early quick judgment regarding the effectiveness of aerobic exercise programs until you have given them considerable time to work. From the standpoint of weight loss, many people expect to lose about a pound every week or so early in the program. Don't quit early! You'll want to lose weight very gradually.

77c Individualized Practice
Key the drill according to the prompts on your screen.

77d WordChamp
Play the game WordChamp.

77e End of Class Procedure . . .
if you are not continuing to the next Session.

Speed Clinic

Were the grandparents handpicked? What is the wisdom in her using an aerosol for the solution? How much was withheld by your boss? It was a jurisdictional dispute. I counted four bathhouses in the old city. Can grandparents do aerobics?

She wants to be an aeronautical engineer. Could anaesthesia make you sick? I will withhold answering that question.

ae	aerosol aegis aerial aerobic aerial anaesthetic larvae vitae
dp	sandpaper floodplains grandparents handpicked standpoints
hh	bathhouses withheld withhold withholding bathhouses withheld
sd	wisdom jurisdiction jurisdictional jurisdictions wisdom

73a ●
Conditioning Practice
Key each exercise at the right three times.

Alphabetic Practice

I live on Augusta Blvd. Where do you play golf? Jack has the moxie to win the quiz.

Digraph Practice (dc oh yz kh tp wy kf)

broadcast prohibit analyze backhoe marketplace lawyer breakfast

73b ● A
Evaluation ~ Analysis
Key the timed writing at the right.

Timed Writing

After analyzing the motion made by one of the stockholders, the new board decided that they would place a ban on the use of alcohol and/or smoking. People opposing this action quickly got a good lawyer and determined several plans of their own. Quick action by the new board to postpone enforcement for several months or more made many of the people very thankful. The board decision was then broadcast on all of the five local radio stations.

73c Individualized Practice
Key the drill according to the prompts on your screen.

73d WordChamp
Play the game WordChamp.

73e End of Class Procedure . . .
if you are not continuing to the next Session.

Speed Clinic

My grandchild likes frankfurters for lunch. R. Law is their lawyer. Oh, look at his footprints. You should analyze and reanalyze the stockholder's request for a postponement.

dc   broadcast grandchild midcities wildcat midcontinent wildcat

oh   oh alcohol prohibit prohibited prohibits prohibitive alcohol

yz   analyze analyzed analyzes analyzing reanalyze reanalyzed

kh   backhaul backhoe stockholder stockholders backhoes backhaul

tp   postpaid output marketplace footprints postpone postponement

wy   lawyer lawyers lawyer lawyers lawyer lawyers lawyer lawyers

kf   breakfast breakfasts frankfurters thankful frankfurters

Refer to page R-1 for tips on efficient keying of individual letters.

76a ●
Conditioning Practice
Key each exercise at the right three times.

Alphabetic Practice
Zane asked what is the purpose of an interview. Bill can just go quickly to the exam.

Digraph Practice (ky ml ku bc dt kd)
skyline lucky firmly backup subcommittee hundredth breakdown

76b ● (HA)
Evaluation ~ Analysis
Key the timed writing at the right.

Timed Writing
Adam was a very young subcontractor and realized early in his career that he got very little exercise on the job. He joined an aerobics group and was firmly committed to participating every other weekday. Adam was a very husky man and had a medical checkup prior to his beginning the program. By the hundredth day of the program, he anticipated considerable weight loss.

76c Individualized Practice
Key the drill according to the prompts on your screen.

76d WordChamp
Play the game WordChamp.

76e End of Class Procedure . . .
if you are not continuing to the next Session.

Speed Clinic

The subcontractors were concerned about the risky breakdown.

The checkup was harmless. Every weekday the bottomlands are flooded. I did a crackdown on the local bookdealers who are selling illegally. What is the width of their streamliner?

ky	skyline junkyard skyrockets bulky lucky husky risky rocky
ml	firmly warmly harmless streamline bottomlands streamliners
ku	backup checkup markup pickup skull skunk backup markup skull
bc	subcommittee subcommittees subcontract subcontractors
dt	breadth hundredth width widths breadth width hundredth width
kd	workday weekday markdowns knockdown crackdown bookdealers

Refer to page **R-1** for tips on efficient keying of individual letters.

Session 74 — Skillbuilding

74a ●
Conditioning Practice
Key each exercise at the right three times.

Alphabetic Practice
Once you have a finalized listing of six quality work goals, make a plan for objectives.

Digraph Practice (ez ux db ej bd hc)
antifreeze auxiliary crux cardboard prejudge subdivide forthcoming

74b ● Ⓐ
Evaluation ~ Analysis
Key the timed writing at the right.

Timed Writing
The board decided the ban on alcohol and/or smoking will still be forthcoming after the postponement. The board did not want to reject the motion, but only to freeze any action until they received feedback from the various subdivisions of the company. Only then will they be able to make a decision that will address the crux of the problem.

74c Individualized Practice
Key the drill according to the prompts on your screen.

74d WordChamp
Play the game WordChamp.

74e End of Class Procedure . . .
if you are not continuing to the next Session.

Speed Clinic

The forthcoming winter means new antifreeze for your car. I want a deluxe handbag. You can rejoice in knowing the plans were rejected for the new subdivision. It was breezy on the luxury sailboat. The roadbed looked like cardboard.

Refer to page R-1 for tips on efficient keying of individual letters.

ez antifreeze freeze sneezed squeeze breezy squeezing freezing

ux deluxe luxury auxiliary auxiliaries luxury influx reflux crux

db cardboard handbag roadbed handbook deadbeat standby feedback

ej reject rejected rejecting rejects rejoice rejoicing prejudge

bd subdivide subdividing subdivision subdivisions subdividing

hc forthcoming forthcoming forthcoming forthcoming forthcoming

75a ●
Conditioning Practice
Key the exercise at the right three times.

Alphabetic Practices

Does Jarvis know the zip code for Albuquerque, New Mexico? Yes, and I think Grover does too.

Which of the following have the letter c in the word: zing, physics, but, exquisite, hawk, jam?

I live on Augusta Blvd. Where do you play golf? Jack has the moxie to win the quiz.

Once you have a finalized listing of six quality work goals, make a plan for objectives.

75b ● Ⓐ
Evaluation ~ Progress
Key the first timed writing at the right.

75c ● Ⓐ
Evaluation ~ Progress
Key the second timed writing at the right.

75d ●
WordChamp
Play the game WordChamp.

75e ●
End of Class Procedure . . .
if you are not continuing to the next Session.

Speed Clinic

Left-Hand Words

Timed Writing

Finding the right job is often not an easy assignment. You will be amazed, however, at the many ways of learning about the right kinds of jobs. A quick way is to use the school placement service or an employment agency. You can expand your search by reading the classified section of your local newspaper. Finally there are the referrals of friends and relatives. In all, you have many choices.

Timed Writing

Even though employers look for certain kinds of qualities and qualifications, each person is different. There is, however, a job for everyone, providing one works to his or her capacity. If a person prepares to the best of his or her ability, there is usually a firm that needs just him or her. Analyze your strengths. Can we expect you to be prepared to the maximum?

When will you test the new tweezers? I read there is a new rebate for our air fare. We have a new logo on our website.

Give our regards to all those who took the test and got high grades. It's no secret that the text was tested and traded.

faded fades fads far fare fares fast faster fat fate freezer

grace grade graded grades graft grass grate grave graze grew

razed razz razzed read readers reads rebate red reef regards

seared secret see seed sees serve served serves set sets sew

tested tests text texts trace trade traded treat treated wet

tweezers wave weave wet waded wars waves web waft wart wages

Reach Techniques

ALPHABET

A   Lightly place the fingertip of the left, fourth (little) finger on the letter **a**. Strike the *a* with a light tap with the fingertip, snapping the fingertip toward your palm.

B   Curl your left, first (f) finger and reach down. Strike the *b* key with a quick snap stroke.

C   Curl your left, second (d) finger and reach down. Stroke the *c* with a quick snap stroke.

D   Lightly place the fingertip of the left, second finger on the letter **d**. Strike the *d* with a light tap with the fingertip, snapping the fingertip toward your palm.

E   Reach up with the left, second (d) finger. Reach up and strike the *e* without moving the hands away from you.

F   Lightly place the fingertip of the left, first finger on the letter **f**. Strike the *f* with a light tap with the fingertip, snapping the fingertip toward your palm.

G   Reach to the right with the left, first (f) finger. Strike the *g* with a quick snap stroke.

H   Reach to the left with the right, first (j) finger. Strike the *h* with a quick snap stroke.

I   Reach up with the right, second (k) finger. Reach up and strike the *i* without moving the hands away from you.

J   Lightly place the fingertip of the right, first finger on the letter **j**. Strike the *j* with a light tap with the fingertip, snapping the fingertip toward your palm.

K   Lightly place the fingertip of the right, second finger on the letter **k**. Strike the *k* with a light tap with the fingertip, snapping the fingertip toward your palm.

L   Lightly place the fingertip of the right, third finger on the letter **l**. Strike the *l* with a light tap with the fingertip, snapping the fingertip toward your palm.

M   Curl your right, first (j) finger and reach down. Strike the *m* with a quick snap stroke.

N   Curl your right, first (j) finger and reach down. Strike the *n* with a quick snap stroke.

O   Reach up with the right, third (l) finger. Reach up and strike the *o* without moving the hands away from you.

P   Reach up with the right, fourth (;) finger. Reach up and strike the *p* without moving the hands away from you.

Q   Reach up with the left, fourth (a) finger. Reach up and strike the *q* without moving the hands away from you.

R   Reach up with the left, first (f) finger. Reach up and strike the *r* without moving the hands.

S   Lightly place the fingertip of the left, third finger on the letter **s**. Strike the *s* with a light tap with the fingertip, snapping the fingertip toward your palm.

T   Reach up with the left, first (f) finger. Reach up and strike the *t* without moving the hands away from you.

U   Reach up with the right, first (j) finger. Reach up and strike the *u* without moving the hands away from you.

V   Curl your left, first (f) finger and reach down. Strike the *v* with a quick snap stroke.

W   Reach up with the left, third (s) finger. Reach up and strike the *w* without moving the hands away from you.

X   Curl your left, third (s) finger and reach down. Strike the *x* with a quick snap stroke.

Y   Reach up with the right, first (j) finger. Reach up and strike the *y* without moving the hands away from you.

Z   Curl your left, fourth (a) finger and reach down. Strike the *z* with a quick snap stroke.

TECHNIQUES FOR OPERATIONS

If one of the following items appears in a diagnosed digraph, the operation will have priority over the other part of the digraph for drill selection.

Double Letters

Be certain to strike the second key with the same force as you struck the first key in the double letter sequence. Use two quick taps of the key.

Concentration

Keep your eyes on the copy, and give your keystroking undivided attention.

Enter

Reach out with the right, little finger. Tap the enter key quickly and return the finger to the home key.

Tab

Reach up and left with the left, fourth (a) finger. Strike the key with a light tap with the fingertip, snapping the fingertip toward your palm.

Left Shift

Reach down and out with the left, fourth (a) finger. Hold the shift key and strike the desired letter. Release both the shift key and the letter key at the same time, and return to home position.

Right Shift

Reach down and out with the right, fourth (;) finger. Hold the shift key and strike the desired letter. Release both the shift key and the letter key at the same time, and return to home position.

Space Bar

Strike the space bar with a quick down-and-in motion of the right thumb. Keep the right thumb above the space bar at all times.

PUNCTUATION AND SYMBOLS

Period (.)

Curl your right, third (l) finger and reach down. Strike the . with a quick snap stroke.

Comma (,)

Curl your right, second (k) finger and reach down. Strike the , with a quick snap stroke.

Question Mark

Press the left shift key. Curl your right, fourth (;) finger and reach down. Strike the ? with a quick snap stroke.

Apostrophe (')

Reach to the right with the right, fourth (;) finger. Strike the ' with a light tap with the fingertip, snapping the fingertip toward your palm.

Quote (")

Press the left shift. Reach to the right with the right, fourth (;) finger. Strike the " with a light tap with the fingertip, snapping the fingertip toward your palm.

Semicolon (;)

Lightly place the tip of the right, fourth (little) finger on the semicolon. Strike the ; with a light tap with the fingertip, snapping the fingertip toward your palm.

Dollar Sign ($)

Press the right shift. Reach up with the left, first (f) finger. Reach up and strike the $ without moving the hands away from you.

Hyphen (-)

Reach up with the right, fourth (;) finger. Reach up and strike the - without moving the hands away from you.

Number Sign (#)

Press the right shift. Reach up with the left, second (d) finger. Reach up and strike the # without moving the hands away from you.

Slash (/)

Curl your right, fourth (;) finger and reach down. Strike the / with a quick snap stroke.

Percent (%)

Press the right shift. Reach up with the left, first (f) finger. Reach up and strike the % without moving the hands away from you.

Underline (_)

Press the left shift. Reach up with the right, fourth (;) finger. Reach up and strike the _ without moving the hands away from you.

Left Parenthesis (()

Press the left shift. Reach up with the right, third (l) finger. Reach up and strike the (without moving the hands away from you.

Right Parenthesis ( ))

Press the left shift. Reach up with the right, fourth (;) finger. Reach up and strike the) without moving the hands away from you.

Ampersand (&)

Press the left shift. Reach up with the right, first (j) finger. Reach up and strike the & without moving the hands away from you.

Colon (:)

Press the left shift. Lightly place the tip of the right, fourth (;) finger on the :. Strike the : with a light tap, snapping the fingertip toward your palm.

Exclamation Point (!)

Press the right shift. Reach up with the left, fourth (a) finger. Reach up and strike the ! without moving the hands away from you.

Asterisk (*)

Press the left shift. Reach up with the right, second (k) finger. Reach up and strike the * without moving the hands away from you.

Plus Sign (+)

Press the left shift. Reach up with the right, fourth (;) finger. Reach up and strike the + without moving the hands away from you.

Equal Sign (=)

Reach up with the right, fourth (;) finger. Reach up and strike the = without moving the hands away from you.

Left Bracket ([)

Reach up with the right, fourth (;) finger. Reach up and strike the [without moving the hands away from you.

Right Bracket (])

Reach up with the right, fourth (;) finger. Reach up and strike the] without moving the hands away from you.

Left Brace ({)

Press the left shift. Reach up with the right, fourth (;) finger. Reach up and strike the { without moving the hands away from you.

Right Brace (})

Press the left shift. Reach up with the right, fourth (;) finger. Reach up and strike the } without moving the hands away from you.

Less Than (<)

Press the left shift. Curl your right, second (k) finger and reach down. Strike the < with a quick snap stroke.

Greater Than (>)

Press the left shift. Curl your right, third (l) finger and reach down. Strike the > with a quick snap stroke.

At Sign (@)

Press the right shift. Reach up with the left, third (s) finger. Reach up and strike the @ without moving the hands away from you.

Tilde (~)

Press the right shift. Reach up with the left, fourth (a) finger. Reach up and strike the ~ without moving the hands away from you.

Grave (`)

Reach up with the left, fourth (a) finger. Reach up and strike the ` without moving the hands away from you.

NUMBERS

If a number is the first part of a digraph, the number is selected for the drill. If two numbers compose the digraph, the second number is selected for the drill.

One (1)

Reach up with the left, fourth (a) finger. Reach up and strike the 1 without moving the hands away from you.

Two (2)

Reach up with the left, third (s) finger. Reach up and strike the 2 without moving the hands away from you.

Three (3)

Reach up with the left, second (d) finger. Reach up and strike the 3 without moving the hands away from you.

Four (4)

Reach up with the left, first (f) finger. Reach up and strike the 4 without moving the hands away from you.

Five (5)

Reach up with the left, first (f) finger. Reach up and strike the 5 without moving the hands away from you.

Six (6)

Reach up with the right, first (j) finger. Reach up and strike the 6 without moving the hands away from you.

Seven (7)

Reach up with the right, first (j) finger. Reach up and strike the 7 without moving the hands away from you.

Eight (8)

Reach up with the right, second (k) finger. Reach up and strike the 8 without moving the hands away from you.

Nine (9)

Reach up with the right, third (l) finger. Reach up and strike the 9 without moving the hands away from you.

Zero (0)

Reach up with the right, fourth (;) finger. Reach up and strike the 0 without moving the hands away from you.

Digraph Index

Digraph	Session	Digraph	Session	Digraph	Session	Digraph	Session	Digraph	Session	Digraph	Session
ab	23	ce	7	ej	74	gu	46	iy	97	lu	36
ac	13	ch	11	ek	51	gw	96	iz	41	lv	53
ad	16	ci	21	el	11	gy	66	ja	72	lw	61
ae	77	ck	31	em	17	ha	3	je	52	ly	14
af	44	cl	26	en	2	hb	68	ji	89	ma	12
ag	26	cn	83	eo	48	hc	74	jo	48	mb	28
ah	66	co	6	ep	23	hd	69	ju	46	mc	97
ai	17	cq	63	eq	36	he	1	ka	62	me	7
aj	63	cr	33	er	1	hf	78	kb	79	mf	68
ak	33	cs	61	es	1	hh	77	kc	87	mi	22
al	7	ct	13	et	11	hi	9	kd	76	ml	76
am	22	cu	31	eu	64	hl	56	ke	27	mm	36
an	2	cy	47	ev	27	hm	63	kf	73	mn	66
ao	87	da	29	ew	31	hn	63	kg	69	mo	21
ap	24	db	74	ex	26	ho	13	kh	73	mp	22
aq	86	dc	73	ey	38	hp	88	ki	38	mr	93
ar	4	dd	44	ez	74	hq	84	kk	79	ms	41
as	7	de	6	fa	32	hr	46	kl	57	mt	92
at	2	df	88	fe	24	hs	56	km	71	mu	39
au	41	dg	53	ff	28	ht	38	kn	44	mv	98
av	16	dh	78	fh	93	hu	53	ko	82	mw	93
aw	49	di	13	fi	16	hw	62	kp	81	my	48
ax	51	dj	62	fl	53	hy	56	kr	86	na	22
ay	21	dk	92	fm	97	ia	24	ks	44	nb	81
az	64	dl	49	fo	6	ib	37	kt	87	nc	12
ba	33	dm	54	fr	29	ic	8	ku	76	nd	3
bb	61	dn	63	fs	67	id	23	kw	82	ne	8
bc	76	do	29	ft	47	ie	19	ky	76	nf	39
bd	74	dp	77	fu	32	if	24	la	13	ng	4
be	9	dq	72	fw	93	ig	27	lb	71	nh	72
bi	37	dr	43	fy	59	ih	91	lc	64	ni	19
bj	58	ds	34	ga	32	ii	86	ld	19	nj	59
bl	21	dt	76	gb	89	ik	48	le	7	nk	36
bm	62	du	28	gd	94	il	8	lf	46	nl	43
bn	83	dv	43	ge	16	im	22	lg	78	nm	57
bo	26	dw	68	gf	81	in	1	lh	96	nn	41
bp	89	dy	51	gg	52	io	6	li	12	no	14
br	44	ea	8	gh	31	ip	32	lk	59	np	67
bs	52	eb	62	gi	33	iq	63	ll	7	nq	57
bt	56	ec	9	gl	52	ir	22	lm	58	nr	66
bu	27	ed	4	gm	67	is	4	ln	69	ns	13
bv	71	ee	12	gn	46	it	3	lo	17	nt	4
bw	89	ef	29	go	37	iu	58	lp	49	nu	37
by	32	eg	33	gr	28	iv	18	lr	61	nv	39
ca	11	eh	57	gs	46	iw	91	ls	34	nw	69
cc	36	ei	29	gt	66	ix	59	lt	43	nx	71

Digraph	Session	Digraph	Session	Digraph	Session	Digraph	Session	Digraph	Session	Digraph	Session
ny	28	pn	83	sg	92	uc	26	wp	88	ze	46
nz	94	po	16	sh	18	ud	42	wr	47	zi	61
oa	42	pp	23	si	11	ue	29	ws	51	zl	83
ob	41	pr	8	sk	49	uf	56	wt	67	zo	69
oc	31	ps	52	sl	54	ug	37	wy	73	zy	98
od	29	pt	38	sm	52	ui	33	xa	56	zz	81
oe	57	pu	39	sn	66	uk	91	xc	51	0	101-102
of	4	pw	83	so	19	ul	17	xe	53	1	101-102
og	42	py	46	sp	28	um	34	xf	99	2	101-102
oh	73	qu	27	sq	69	un	17	xh	68	3	101-102
oi	41	ra	8	sr	72	uo	59	xi	53	4	103-104
oj	58	rb	58	ss	14	up	31	xl	81	5	103-104
ok	43	rc	36	st	3	uq	96	xo	99	6	103-104
ol	21	rd	22	su	17	ur	3	xp	42	7	106-107
om	11	re	1	sv	99	us	12	xq	99	8	106-107
on	2	rf	56	sw	57	ut	18	xs	98	9	106-107
oo	23	rg	42	sy	51	uu	84	xt	46	@	108-109
op	19	rh	61	ta	9	uv	81	xu	88	$	108-109
oq	98	ri	12	tb	72	ux	74	xy	79	#	109
or	2	rj	98	tc	62	uy	59	ya	61	\	111
os	16	rk	38	td	79	uz	97	yb	71	%	112
ot	17	rl	48	te	3	va	34	yc	69	^	112
ou	1	rm	28	tf	64	ve	6	yd	72	&	112
ov	27	rn	32	tg	63	vi	18	ye	34	*	113-114
ow	18	ro	9	th	1	vo	43	yf	97	()	113-114
ox	54	rp	48	ti	2	vu	92	yg	82	_	116
oy	47	rq	94	tl	39	vy	66	yh	71	"	116
oz	67	rr	36	tm	44	wa	23	yi	54	,	116
pa	14	rs	13	tn	68	wb	84	yl	64	-	117
pb	86	rt	14	to	3	wc	91	ym	49	=	117
pc	88	ru	38	tp	73	wd	79	yn	78	'	117
pd	87	rv	36	tr	18	we	8	yo	6	/	118
pe	11	rw	51	ts	18	wf	83	yp	54	[]	119
pf	64	ry	24	tt	22	wh	19	yr	66	{}	121-122
pg	86	sa	26	tu	24	wi	9	ys	42	<	123-124
ph	47	sb	71	tw	44	wk	92	yt	62	>	123-124
pi	34	sc	34	ty	26	wl	58	yu	96	?	123
pk	94	sd	77	tz	94	wm	78	yw	68	!	123
pl	14	se	6	ua	31	wn	43	yz	73	:	124
pm	48	sf	53	ub	28	wo	23	za	53		